DDD
PRISM
SERIES
Volume 6

Embedded Instruction
for Students With Developmental Disabilities in General Education Classrooms

by John McDonnell,
Jesse W. Johnson,
and Camille McQuivey

D1508907

A Publication of the Division
on Developmental Disabilities
of the Council for Exceptional Children

Council for
Exceptional
Children
The voice and vision of special education

TABLE OF CONTENTS

Appendices

CHAPTER

1

Embedded Instruction in General Education Classes

The number of students with developmental disabilities served in general education classes has steadily increased over the last decade (U. S. Department of Education, 2004). Research consistently has shown that inclusive educational programs produce positive educational and social outcomes for all students, both with and without disabilities (Hunt & McDonnell, 2007). However, including students with developmental disabilities in general education classes and the general education curriculum also presents a number of challenges to teachers. Perhaps one of the most significant challenges is providing systematic instruction that is tailored to students' unique needs while still compatible with the typical teaching approaches used in general education classes (Harrower, 1999; McDonnell, 1998). One strategy that has been shown to be particularly effective in addressing these two issues is *Embedded Instruction* (EI) (Hunt & McDonnell, 2007; Snell, 2007).

Although there is no widely accepted definition of EI (Rule et al., 1998; Schepis, Reid, Ownbey, & Parsons, 2001; Wolery, Ault, & Doyle, 1992), the term commonly refers to explicit, systematic instruction designed to distribute instructional trials within the on-going routines and activities of the performance environment. The specific instructional procedures used during EI vary based on (a) the needs of the individual student, (b) the skill being taught, and (c) the context in which instruction is being provided.

Several approaches to EI emerged in the 1970s and 1980s as a way to teach language

Insights From the Experts

Fantuzzo and Atkins (1992) noted the pressing need for special educators and applied behavior analysts to "develop more adaptive and effective strategies to promote academic and social competency, and develop strategies that teachers and school personnel *can* and *will* actually use." (p. 37; italics in original). Further, they observed that "there is no rigorous behavior-analytic technology that reflects an appreciation for the factors involved in entering complex school systems" (p. 38).

and social skills to students with developmental disabilities within the context of typical home, school, and community settings. These included incidental teaching (Hart & Risely, 1968, 1974, 1975); mand-model (Warren, McQuarter, Rogers-Warren, 1984); milieu teaching (Kaiser, Hendrickson, & Alper, 1991); naturalistic time delay (Halle, Baer, & Spradlin, 1981; Halle, Marshall, & Spradlin, 1979; Schwarts, Anderson, & Halle, 1989); pivotal response training (Koegel, O'Dell, & Koegel, 1987; Pierce & Schreibman, 1995, 1997); and chain-interruption (Alwell, Hunt, Goetz, & Sailor, 1989; Goetz, Gee, & Sailor, 1985; Gee, Graham, Goetz, Oshima, & Yoshioka, 1991; Hunt, Goetz, Alwell, & Sailor, 1986).

During the 1980s and 1990s, other EI strategies emerged as a way to teach other academic and developmental skills to students within typical routines to make them more functional, and to promote generalization and maintenance of these skills. These strategies included activity-based instruction (Ford et al., 1989; Holvet & Brown, 1980; Lasardo & Bricker, 1994; Wilcox & Bellamy, 1987); the curriculum sequencing model (Guess & Sailor, 1986); and transition-based teaching (Werts, Wolery, Holcombe, Vasilaros, & Phillips, 1992).

Although there is a significant amount of research demonstrating the effectiveness of various EI teaching approaches, the vast majority of the early studies were conducted with preschool children with developmental disabilities or who were in separate special education settings. One notable exception was a study conducted by Wolery, Anthony, Snyder, Werts, and Katzenmeyer (1997). They taught general education teachers to use embedded instruction with three students with severe disabilities who were included in typical elementary classes. The teachers used a constant time delay procedure to embed instruction for students within the lessons being provided to typical students in the class. The skills that were taught included reading sight words during language

Box 1-1: Teaching Mark to Write His Name

Mark is included in Mrs. Swanson's first grade class. One of his individualized education program (IEP) goals is to learn to write his first name. Mrs. Swanson and Mrs. Hansen, Mark's special education teacher, decided to use embedded instruction to teach him this skill. Together, they decided that they could provide Mark at least two opportunities during each lesson throughout the day by requiring him to write his name on worksheets, workbook pages, and project materials. Mrs. Hansen developed an embedded instruction teaching plan that began with Mark being provided with a model and Mrs. Swanson providing physical assistance to help him write the letters. The model and assistance were slowly faded across instructional sessions. Mrs. Swanson arranged her schedule so that she could help Mark at least twice during each lesson. After less than a month of instruction, Mark has learned to write his first name and now is working on last name.

Chapter 1. Embedded Instruction in General Education Classes

arts instruction, naming the days of the week on which selected activities occurred during opening activities, and categorizing specific foods within the appropriate food group during science class. Results showed that students learned the targeted skills, and general educators were able to successfully implement embedded instruction within activities of the general education class.

Previous research on EI suggested that it held promise as an approach for providing effective instruction to students with developmental disabilities enrolled in general education classes. Over the last several years, we have conducted a series of studies to determine if EI could meet the learning needs of students in inclusive settings and to identify the mix of teaching strategies that would optimize its effectiveness. The purpose of this book is to share what we have learned to date about EI. Clearly, more research is needed. However, the cumulative results of our studies to date indicate that it is a useful approach for enhancing learning for students with developmental disabilities who are included in general education classes.

In this chapter we will provide a more detailed definition of EI, review the research studies that we have completed on EI, and provide an overview of a process that teachers can use to design EI in general education classes. The remaining chapters provide step-by-step directions for implementing EI.

Definition of Embedded Instruction

As discussed, a number of instructional approaches designed to distribute instructional trials within the on-going routines and activities of performance environments have been examined over the last several decades. Various labels have been used, including "naturalistic instruction," "incidental teaching," and "embedded instruction" to differentiate these instructional approaches from the kind of discrete trial instruction that often occurs in traditional separate special education programs (Hepting & Goldstein, 1996; Rule et al., 1998; Wolery et al., 1992). Researchers and teachers working with preschool children with disabilities typically use the term *naturalistic instruction* to refer to these strategies. A key procedural element of naturalistic instruction is that the interaction between the teacher and the child follows the child's lead or interest (Rule et al.).

For example, if a child was playing in a dress up area and he/she reached for a hat that the teacher was holding, the teacher would take the child's reach as an opportunity to prompt a verbal response by saying, "What do you want?" and then providing a verbal model ("Hat"). Although we believe that teachers should take advantage of all student initiated opportunities for instruction, preschool classes for young children are typically more dynamic and fluid than classes for school-age children. Thus, child-lead teaching opportunities are likely to be more consistently available in preschool classes than in classes for school-age children.

The more structured nature of general education classes requires that instruction be teacher-lead with instructional trials being specifically planned and scheduled during each lesson. Consequently, we prefer the term *embedded instruction*. EI is characterized by several critical features.

- *The expected learning outcomes for the student in the general education class are clearly delineated.* The teacher has developed explicit goals and objectives for the student and specific criteria for judging the effectiveness of EI on student learning have been established.

- *Instruction is designed to accommodate the presence or absence of "natural" instructional trials within typical routines or activities.* Prior to instruction, the teacher analyzes the typical routines and activities of the general education class to identify when and how often opportunities to teach the target skill occur naturally within the usual classroom routines or activities. If natural teaching opportunities occur inconsistently, then the teacher should identify specific opportunities when supplemental examples might be presented to the student to promote efficient learning.

- *Instructional trials are distributed within or across the typical routines or activities in the general education class.* In traditional teaching arrangements instructional trials are presented one after another within a teaching session. In contrast, EI trials are separated in time and distributed across routines and activities.

- *The number and time of delivery of instructional trials is planned and scheduled within each routine and activity.* The teacher creates a schedule for the delivery of instructional trials that ensures efficient learning and minimizes the disruption of EI to classroom activities and interactions.

- *Instruction is based on empirically validated instructional procedures.* The teacher utilizes response prompting and fading procedures that minimize errors during the initial stages of acquisition, corrects errors consistently, and builds on the natural reinforcers available within the classroom.

- *Instructional decisions are driven by student performance data.* Data on the student's acquisition of the target skills are collected regularly, with the teacher using these data to make modifications to the teaching plan in order to maximize its efficacy.

Research on Embedded Instruction in General Education Classes

To date, we have completed 10 studies examining EI as a strategy for supporting student learning in general education classes. In this section, we summarize our research on the effectiveness of EI, compare EI and traditional instructional approaches, and examine key procedural elements of EI.

Demonstrations of Effectiveness

The four studies we have completed on the effectiveness of EI focused on three questions. The first question was to determine whether EI would produce consistent student learning when it was implemented within the on-going routines and activities of general education classes. Two of the studies were conducted in elementary classes and two were conducted in middle school content-area classes.

The second question was whether EI could be successfully implemented by teachers, paraeducators, and peers. In two studies, EI was conducted by general educators. In a third study, EI was implemented by paraeducators who were assigned to support participation of the students with developmental disabilities in the instructional activities of the general education classes. In another study, students without disabilities were trained to implement EI with their peers with developmental disabilities. The third and final question was to determine whether the individuals implementing EI thought that it was an effective and acceptable approach to support the participation of students with disabilities in general education classes.

To help answer these questions, Johnson, McDonnell, Holzwarth, and Hunter (2004) used a multiple baseline across behaviors design to evaluate the efficacy of embedded instruction with three students with developmental disabilities who were enrolled in general education classes. Two general education teachers and one paraprofessional delivered embedded instruction to students during regularly scheduled instructional activities. The skills taught to students included (a) answering probe questions drawn from the regular science curriculum, (b) identifying functional sight-words drawn from the regular reading curriculum, and (c) making requests using an electronic communication device. The data showed that embedded instruction was effective with all three students. The results also indicate that both general education teachers and the paraprofessional were able to implement the procedure with a high degree of fidelity without disrupting the ongoing instructional activities of the general education classes. Teacher ratings of the acceptability and perceived effectiveness of the procedures suggested that they viewed embedded instruction as a practical, effective, and efficient strategy for teaching students with developmental disabilities in general education settings.

McDonnell et al. (2002) used a multiple baseline across behaviors design to evaluate the efficacy of embedded instruction with four junior high school students with developmental disabilities. The study was designed to examine whether paraprofessional staff could successfully implement EI as part of their responsibilities in supporting the participation of students in the class. In addition, the study focused on teaching skills drawn directly from (a) the general education curriculum, and (b) the lessons being presented to students without disabilities. Students were taught to read or define words that were included on vocabulary lists of several general education classes including a food and nutrition class, a health class, and a computer class. EI was carried out by special education paraprofessional staff assigned to support the students in their classes. The results indicated that embedded instruction led to the acquisition and maintenance of the target skills. The paraprofessionals implemented the embedded instruction procedures in general education classes with high levels of procedural fidelity. The students' general education teachers and the paraprofessionals reported that EI was an effective and acceptable strategy for supporting their participation in the general education curriculum.

Jameson and McDonnell (2007) taught three junior high school students without disabilities to deliver EI to three peers with developmental disabilities in their general education classes. The purpose of the study was to determine if peers without disabilities enrolled in the same class could successfully implement EI with students with developmental disabilities, and whether they could generalize the implementation of EI to similar instructional activities without assistance or feedback. Two of the students with developmental disabilities were enrolled in an arts and crafts class and the third was enrolled in a health class. The students were taught to define key concepts drawn from the lessons being presented to students without disabilities enrolled in the classes. Students without disabilities were taught to implement EI in a 30-min training session prior to the implementation of the study and were provided on-going feedback about their implementation of EI on one set of concepts throughout the study. The students were also asked to implement the EI procedures with another set of concepts for which they received no assistance or feedback. The results showed that students with developmental disabilities learned the target skills when receiving instruction from peers without disabilities. The results also demonstrated that peers without disabilities could implement EI with a high degree of procedural fidelity, and successfully generalize the implementation of EI to similar instructional activities without assistance or feedback. Finally, the students without disabilities and their general education teachers reported that EI was an effective and acceptable strategy for providing instruction to students within the on-going routines of the general education classes.

The results of these studies are consistent with the findings of the study conducted by Wolery et al. (1997) and an initial exploratory study conducted by Johnson and McDonnell (2004). Briefly, these studies suggested that EI is an effective strategy for teaching skills to elementary and middle school age students that are drawn either from their IEP or from the general education curriculum. The general educators, paraprofessionals, and peers without disabilities who participated in the studies learned to implement EI with a limited amount of training and on-going support. These studies also concluded that while EI consistently produced student learning, it is also perceived by teachers, paraprofessionals, and peers as being an acceptable approach compatible with the typical instructional activities of general education classes.

Although these studies demonstrated that EI was effective, a primary question was whether it was as effective as traditional instructional approaches with students with developmental disabilities. It is not uncommon for students to receive parallel instruction using traditional one-to-one instructional formats in general education classes, or to receive one-to-one or small group pull-out instruction on the content of the general education classes in their special education class. The rationale for providing this kind of instruction is that students may not master content-area knowledge solely through the instructional activities provided by the general education teacher. It has been suggested that parallel or pullout instructional approaches can create social separation of students with developmental disabilities and their peers without disabilities (Downing, 1996; Ryndak & Alper, 2003). Ideally, the instruction provided to students with disabilities should be as unobtrusive as possible, and blend with the instructional activities provided by the general educator.

McDonnell et al. (2006) compared the effectiveness of embedded instruction in general education classes and small-group instruction in special education classes to teach vocabulary word definitions to four middle school students with developmental disabilities. In addition, this study examined the extent to which the two instructional formats led to the generalization of students' performance to materials typically used in the general education classes (i.e., teacher developed worksheets, textbooks). Embedded instruction was implemented with four middle school students in their seventh and ninth grade science classes, specifically in health classes and history classes. Students were taught to verbally define five vocabulary words obtained from the general curriculum. Instructional trials were distributed within and across the ongoing activities of the general education class. Instructional procedures included constant time-delay, differential reinforcement, and systematic error correction procedures. Small-group instruction was implemented in the students' self-contained special education class. Students were taught to verbally define five vocabulary words drawn from the curriculum in their general education classes. Instructional procedures for small-group instruction were identical to those used during embedded instruction. The small-groups included the target student and two peers who were randomly selected from his or her special education class. Small-group instruction employed an intrasequential format with spaced-trials (Collins et al., 1991; Reid & Favell, 1984). The results showed that embedded and small-group instruction were equally effective in promoting the acquisition and generalization of the target skill.

Jameson et al. (2007) compared the relative effectiveness of one-on-one embedded instruction in general educations classrooms with one-on-one massed-trial instruction in a special education class with four middle school students with developmental disabilities. EI was implemented with one student in his foods class, with two other students in their teen living classes, and with a final student in his earth science class. Three of the students were taught to identify or define key concepts drawn from the general education curriculum and the lessons presented to students without disabilities. The final student was taught to identify cooking symbols that were drawn from a picture cooking curriculum that would allow him to complete cooking activities in his foods class. The results indicate that both instructional formats were effective in promoting the acquisition of the target skills. However, the data showed that one-to-one massed-trial instruction was slightly more effective for two of the students, one-to-one embedded instruction was more effective for one student, and the two strategies were equally effective for the last student.

Although additional research is needed on this issue, the two studies that we have completed showed that EI was as effective, if not more effective, for six of the eight students participating in the studies. The studies raise questions about the need for parallel or pull-out instruction for most students with developmental disabilities enrolled in general education classes. Until more information about the factors that influence student learning in EI versus traditional instructional formats is gathered, we would recommend that teachers adhere to the "principle of parsimony" in designing instruction for students in general education classes (Etzel & LeBlanc, 1979). That is, if two approaches are equally effective then the teacher should start with the simplest and least intrusive intervention first, and modify teaching procedures as necessary to accommodate the student's learning needs. Based on the studies we have completed, we would support beginning with EI to teach skills to most students. If they do not progress adequately, then the teacher could consider supplementing EI with parallel instruction in the general education class using traditional formats. Finally, pull-out instruction should be viewed as appropriate in situations where less intrusive options are ineffective.

Key Procedural Components

EI should be designed to incorporate empirically validated instructional strategies. The first critical component of EI is the response prompting and fading procedure used to provide assistance to students. The response prompting and fading procedure used by the teacher can have a significant impact on the effectiveness of EI and its compatibility with the ongoing routines and activities of the class. All of the aforementioned studies that documented the effectiveness of

EI used a constant time delay procedure to provide assistance to students. Our research went on to compare various response prompting and fading procedures within EI format.

A second critical component of EI is how instructional trials are distributed within or across classroom routines and activities. We have completed one study examining this issue. The following sections summarize the results of these studies.

Response prompting and fading procedures. One of the most important components of any teaching plan is the response prompting and fading procedure used by the teacher to support student learning (Westling & Fox, 2004; Wolery et al., 1992). The purpose of response prompting is to help the student make the correct response during the initial stages of instruction. A number of response prompting and fading procedures have been shown to be effective with students with developmental disabilities including time delay, the system of most prompts, the system of least prompts, and more recently simultaneous prompting (Wolery et al., 1992). As indicated previously, most of the studies examining the effectiveness of EI utilized a constant time-delay (CTD) procedure to teach skills to students participating in the studies.

We selected and implemented the CTD procedure because (a) it has been used successfully to teach a wide range of skills to students with developmental disabilities, (b) studies comparing CTD with other strategies have generally found it to be more effective, and (c) it is easy to use and only requires the teacher to remember whether the prompt should be provided immediately to the student or delayed for a specified period of time (Schuster et al., 1998; Wolery et al., 1992). Although CTD was an effective strategy in our studies, it was not clear whether other strategies could be implemented efficiently within an EI format or whether they were more or less effective in producing student learning. Consequently, we designed and implemented a series of three studies to compare various response prompting and fading procedures within an EI format.

The first two studies were designed to compare constant time delay with simultaneous prompting and the system of least prompts. Simultaneous prompting and the system of least prompts were chosen because of their demonstrated effectiveness in teaching discrete skills to students with developmental disabilities (Demchak, 1990; Doyle, Wolery, Ault, & Gast, 1988; Morse & Schuster, 2004). However, we were also interested in examining strategies that would be easy for professionals (general educators and paraprofessionals) or peers who have little technical expertise to provide systematic instruction to students in general education classes. Simultaneous prompting provides potential advantages in this area because it does not require the instructor to change either the type of prompt provided to the student or the temporal proximity of the prompt to the discriminative stimulus. The system of least prompts might provide some advantage because the instructor only provides assistance after the student makes an error and then implements a prescribe hierarchy of prompts until the student gives the desired response.

The final study in the series compared the relative effectiveness of simultaneous prompting and the system of most prompts. These two procedures were selected because of their overall effectiveness and because there has been little research examining their utility in providing instruction to students in general education classes.

Riesen, McDonnell, Johnson, Polychronis, and Jameson (2003) compared CTD time delay and simultaneous prompting procedures within an EI format to teach academic skills to four middle school students with developmental disabilities. The CTD procedure was divided into two sequential steps. In the first step, typically referred to as the "zero-delay" step, the teacher provides a prompt to the student to complete the correct response immediately after the instructional cue or task direction. The teacher's prompt is faded in the second step by delaying the teacher's prompt by a prespecified amount of following the instructional cue or task direction. The simultaneous prompting procedure is similar to CTD in that the teacher provides the prompt to the student immediately after the instructional cue or task direction. However, no attempt is made to fade the teacher's prompt. Instead, prior to the prompted trials, the teacher conducts a test to determine if the student can independently perform the skill. Instruction is stopped when the student demonstrates skill mastery during the test probes.

In this study, instruction was provided by the paraprofessionals who supported these students in their general education classes. The instructional targets were for the students to read or define key vocabulary words extracted from the curriculum in a general education class. Instruction was carried out in 2 seventh-grade science classes, an eighth-grade German language class, and a ninth-grade history class. The paraprofessionals used CTD to teach one set of vocabulary words and simultaneous prompting to teach another set. The number of instructional trials provided to students was controlled under both conditions. The results of the study showed that both procedures were effective in promoting the acquisition of the target skills. However, the CTD procedure was more effective for two of the students and the simultaneous prompting procedure was more effective for the remaining students. The paraprofessionals were to implement embedded instruction with a high degree of procedural fidelity regardless of the response prompting and fading procedure used.

Johnson, McDonnell, and Holzwarth (2007) compared the effectiveness of CTD and the system of least prompts in teaching basic academic skills to four elementary students with developmental disabilities. Two general education teachers and two paraprofessionals provided EI using CTD and the system of least prompts to the students in their general education classrooms. In the system of least prompts, the student is given an opportunity to respond to the target stimulus. If he or she fails to respond or does not respond within an appropriate time period, the teacher provides increasing levels of assistance until they complete the correct response (Wolery et al., 1992). The procedural elements of the system of least prompts have varied in published research studies (Doyle et al., 1988) but typically include a prespecified hierarchy of prompts and the delivery of reinforcement when the student correctly completes the target response. The system of least prompts has been widely recommended as a strategy for teaching students with developmental disabilities (Snell & Brown, 2000; Westling & Fox, 2004) and has been used success-fully to teach a diverse set of skills ranging from reading community shopping words to table cleaning (Bates & Renzaglia, 1982; Colyer, & Collins, 1996; Duker & Morsink, 1984; Jones & Collins, 1997; Smith, Collins, Schuster, & Kleinert, 1999; Test, Rossi, & Kuel, 1988).

Collins, Branson, Hall, and Rankin (2001) used a system of least prompts within a parallel instructional format to teach three students with developmental disabilities to write letters within a general education 12th-grade English class. The general educator and peer tutors who worked with the students in the special education class were taught to implement the system of least prompts in the general education class. Instruction on the letter writing task was conducted simultaneously with the instructional activities provided to students without disabilities. The results indicated that the system of least prompts was effective in teaching the target skill to the students with developmental disabilities. The general education teacher and the peer tutors implemented the procedure with a high degree of fidelity. However, the reports from the general education teacher about the instruction procedures employed in the study were mixed.

In our study, one student was taught to respond to oral questions from the general education social studies curriculum, another student was taught addition and subtraction facts, and two students were taught the sounds associated with letter and letter combinations. Data on student responses indicated that both CTD and system of least prompts were effective in teaching the targeted skills. However, the CTD procedure was slightly more efficient (in terms of trials to criterion) for three of the four students. The results indicated that the general education teachers and paraprofessionals were able to implement both procedures with a high degree of fidelity. In addition, teacher ratings of the effectiveness and acceptability of both procedures were high.

Johnson, McDonnell, Holzwarth, and Berry (2007) compared the efficacy of the simultaneous prompting and the system of most prompts to teach three elementary students with developmental disabilities. Two paraprofessionals implemented simultaneous prompting and the system of most prompts within an EI format in the students' general education classes. In the system of most prompts, the intensity of prompts provided to the student is reduced systematically across instructional trials or sessions as he or she is able to complete the target response more independently (Wolery et al., 1992).

As in simultaneous prompting, the discriminative stimulus and the controlling prompts are paired to minimize the number of errors that students make during instruction. The initial prompt is selected to elicit a correct response from the student during instruction. The intensity of the prompt is reduced when the student meets a prespecified performance criterion. The teacher continues to reduce the level of assistance provided to the student until she or he can complete the target response independently.

The system of most prompts has been effective in teaching students with developmental disabilities a wide range of skills (Batu, Erenekon, Erbas, & Akmanoglu, 2004; Cuvo, Jacobi, & Sipko, 1981; Duker & Morsink, 1984; Kayser, Billingsely, & Neel, 1986; King & Mace, 1990; Massey & Wheeler, 2000). Unfortunately, it has not received a significant amount of attention as a strategy for providing effective instruction to students enrolled in general education classes. Hall, McClannahan, and Krantz (1995) examined the use of a system of most prompts to teach the use of picture activity schedules by students with developmental disabilities participating in elementary classes. The use of the schedules was taught by three paraprofessionals who supported the children's participation in instructional activities. The intervention led to increased levels of task engagement by all of the students. The paraprofessionals reported high levels of satisfaction with the instructional procedures.

In our study, two students were taught to read and define words associated with the third-grade general education geography curriculum and the third student was taught to answer oral questions from a general education science unit on trees. The results showed that both procedures led to the acquisition of the target skills for all three students. For two students, the system of most prompts was more efficient in terms of rate of acquisition and number of trials to criterion. Simultaneous prompting was slightly more efficient in terms of trials to criterion for the third student. The paraprofessionals were able to implement both procedures with a high degree of fidelity, and rated both procedures as equally effective and efficient.

Collectively these studies demonstrate that a variety of response prompting and fading procedures can be used effectively within EI. As in traditional instructional formats, the teacher should select a response prompting and fading strategy that (a) meets the student's learning; (b) matches the demands of the target behavior; (c) can be easily and consistently implemented by the instructor carrying out EI; and (d) will be acceptable to the student, peers, and professionals working in the general education class (Wolery et al., 1992).

Distribution of instructional trials. A key feature of EI is the distribution of instructional trials within and/or across classroom routines and activities (McDonnell, 1998; Wolery, 2002). Although there is no commonly accepted definition of distributed trial training, it is frequently characterized as the interspersing of instructional trials for one task among other training trials for other tasks during an instructional session (Bambara & Warren, 1992; Hepting & Goldstein, 1996; Mulligan, Lacey, & Guess 1982; Westling & Fox, 2004). In EI, the instructional trials on the skill being taught are interspersed within the instruction being provided by the general education teacher to all students in the class.

Previous research on distributed trial instruction has found the strategy to be effective with students with developmental disabilities (Bambara, Warren, & Komisar, 1988; Dunlap & Dunlap, 1987; Mulligan et al., 1982; Winterling, Dunlap, & O'Neill, 1987; Wolery, Anthony, Caldwell, Snyder, & Morgante, 2002). Although research on distributed trial training has been favorable, there is little information about how key features of distributed trial training such as the length of time between trials, the number of trials provided during instructional sessions, and the number of activities in which the trials are embedded influence student learning. Further, there are no studies that have directly assessed how these features of distributed trial instruction can be structured to be compatible with the typical structure of general education classes. To date, we have completed one study examining these issues.

Polychronis, McDonnell, Johnson, Riesen, and Jameson (2004) examined the effectiveness of two trial distribution schedules implemented in an embedded instruction package to teach academic skills to four elementary students with developmental disabilities in general education classes. Students were taught to (a) name numbers from one to nine, (b) identify the teacher and five classmates by name, (c) name the capital of 20 states when presented with the state name, and (d) tell time at 15 and 30 minutes past the hour. In the first package, instructional trials were distributed across a 30-min time period that reflected the typical length of a lesson in the content area (e.g., math or reading). In the second package, instructional trials were distributed across a 120-min time period that cut across at least two lessons (e.g., math and reading). General education teachers provided instruction to students under both trial distribution conditions. The results indicated that both schedules lead to the acquisition of the target skills. In addition, students were able to generalize their performance to natural stimuli found in general education classes. However, the 30-min trial distribution schedule resulted in faster acquisition of the skills for two of the students. There were no substantial differences in the rates of acquisition under the two schedules for the other two students. In analyzing the data more closely, we found that the two students with more significant disabilities learned the skills more quickly when the trials were distributed with a 30-min schedule than when they were distributed over a longer time period. The results also showed that the general education teachers were able to

---

implement EI with a high degree of fidelity under both conditions. Furthermore, the teachers viewed the utility and acceptability of EI favorably regardless of the trial distribution schedule used.

The results of this study do not allow us to make firm recommendations concerning the distribution of instructional trials within or across routines and activities. At this point, this decision should be based on factors such as whether the target skill logically fits with activities, and if there are a sufficient number of "natural" opportunities to receive instruction on a skill across the school day. Some skills (e.g., learning to write one's first name) would fit logically with many instructional activities. In most classes there would be numerous opportunities for the student to receive instruction. However, instruction on other skills (such as doing double digit addition) might more reasonably be carried out during the math lesson. Other issues that should be considered, and will be discussed in more detail later in the guide, are the number of opportunities to provide instruction during a routine or activity, and whether providing EI on a particular skill might disrupt the on-going flow of instruction in the general education class.

Summary

Previous research and our own work has indicated that EI is an effective approach for supporting student learning in general education classes. Our studies have shown that EI (a) can be implemented in both elementary and middle school classes, (b) can be used to teach students with a wide range of abilities and skills, (c) can be used to teach a variety of academic and developmental skills, and (d) is perceived by professionals and peers as an effective and compatible with the instructional routines and activities of general education classes. Successfully including students in general education classes will require teachers to implement a wide array of strategies (Hunt & McDonnell, 2007). EI should be viewed by teachers as just one tool for meeting the needs of students in these settings.

In Chapter 2, we lay out the specific steps of the process and introduce case studies that will be used to illustrate the steps through out the book. Subsequent chapters provide specific directions on how to complete each step of the process. In addition, we include a number of forms that teachers can use to implement the steps of the process.

CHAPTER

2

Overview of Embedded Instruction

This chapter is designed to provide step-by-step directions for the design and implementation of EI with students with developmental disabilities in general education classes. This work is based on two assumptions. First, EI will only be effective if special and general educators work together to meet the educational needs of the student. EI incorporates a number of teaching strategies that most special educators know about and use in other instructional settings. This knowledge is critical to the overall effectiveness of EI in meeting a student's needs. However, if EI is going to be used to maximize students' successful participation in the general education class and the general education curriculum, the knowledge of general educators and their participation in the design and implementation of EI is critical to its success.

Second, EI should be viewed as only one small piece of the student's educational program in general education classes. Other significant elements include the use of differentiated curriculum strategies, the use of adaptations and accommodations to allow the student to participate successfully in all instructional activities, and personal supports to allow full participation in the general education class (Hunt & McDonnell, 2007). In addition, many students will also require direct instruction in traditional one-to-one or small group formats. The challenge facing teachers is how to combine and integrate EI with other instructional strategies to allow the student to succeed in school.

Steps in the Process

Figure 2-1 presents a flow chart outlining the basic steps of developing and implementing EI for a student enrolled in a general education class. The steps include (a) prepare for instruction, (b) design the EI program, (c) implement the program, and (d) support ongoing student learning. Each step is further divided into specific activities that teachers must complete in order to successfully implement EI. We provide an overview of each of these steps in the following sections, and subsequent chapters will explain each in greater detail.

Figure 2-1

A Process for Designing and Implementing Embedded Instruction

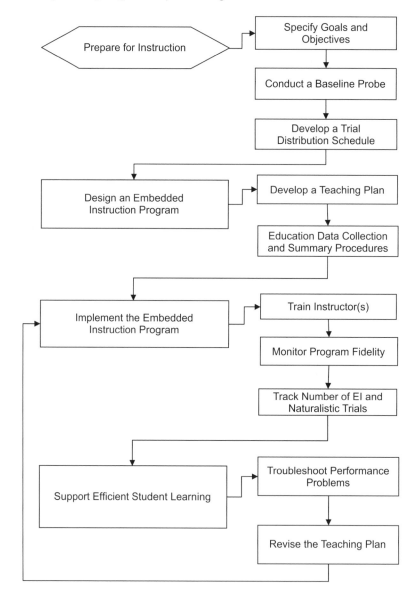

Step 1: Prepare for Instruction

The first activity required to prepare for EI is to identify the learning goals and objectives for the student's participation in the general education class. These goals and objectives can be obtained from the general education curriculum or from the student's individualized education program (IEP). A key here is to collaborate with the student's general education teacher to identify the goals and objectives to be addressed through EI.

The second activity is to conduct a baseline probe of the student's performance on the goal or objective. The baseline probe establishes the student's level of performance prior to instruction so the effectiveness of the EI teaching plan can be evaluated. In addition, the information gathered during the baseline probe will be used to design the EI teaching plan so that it is tailored to the student's individual learning needs.

Finally, the teacher must develop a trial distribution schedule. This activity focuses on identifying opportunities to provide EI during on-going classroom routines and activities. In addition, it allows the teacher to systematically plan the specific times when EI trials are presented to the student.

Step 2: Design an Embedded Instruction Program

The first task here is to structure the teaching plan to ensure that key components of the teaching interaction are clearly articulated prior to the beginning of EI. These components include (a) the times at which instructional trials are presented to the student, (b) the specific instructional examples that are presented during the trials, (c) the response prompts provided to the student to ensure correct responding, and (d) the steps for correcting student errors and reinforcing correct responses. The specificity of the teaching plan is critical in ensuring that EI is consistently delivered across all individuals who are serving as instructors. In addition, the scripted nature of the teaching plan is intended to provide maximum support to individuals who may not have experience in providing instruction to individuals with developmental disabilities.

The second critical task in this step is the development of data collection and summary procedures. The process uses regularly scheduled "probes" to assess student performance in the EI teaching plan. This provides an independent and reliable means of assessing student progress and to reduce the demands on instructors who are trying to implement EI within the on-going routines and activities of the classroom.

Step 3: Implement the EI Program

The best teaching plan will only be effective if the individuals implementing the plan reliably follow the procedures laid out by the teacher. Consequently, effectively training instructors to implement the teaching plan is vital. The long-term success of EI is enhanced if the teacher systematically monitors the correct implementation of the teaching plan by the individuals implementing it. This activity involves regular observation of and feedback to the instructors.

Finally, the teaching plan will only be successful if the student receives an adequate number of instructional trials each day. This can be determined either by the teacher during their regular observations of the instructors, or by asking the instructors to track the number and type of instructional trials provided to the student during each lesson.

Step 4: Support Efficient Student Learning

No teaching plan is perfect. Teachers must regularly examine the student's performance during probe sessions to determine whether changes in the teaching strategies are needed. This examination should focus on the specific errors that the student is making, followed by the development of a hypothesis for why the student is making these errors.

Case Studies

Each step in this process can be more completely explained and illustrated through the use of case studies. Here are two typical situations.

Jacob

Jacob is a 15-year-old ninth grader with moderate intellectual disabilities. Jacob communicates using two to three word sentences, with difficulty articulating some words. He attends his neighborhood junior high school and is enrolled in several general education classes during the day. One of the classes is a foods and nutrition class taken by ninth graders. Prior to his IEP meeting, Jacobs's special education teacher and his foods and nutrition teacher met to discuss specific goals and objectives for him in that class. The district curriculum for the class requires that all students be able to read, define, and apply a number of concepts in planning and preparing balanced and nutritious meals. Jacob's teachers identified several skills from the curriculum that would be appropriate for him, and would enhance both his participation in the class and his ability to prepare meals at home.

One of the skills that they identified was to read words or symbols that he could use to follow recipes. Ultimately, his IEP team decided that this skill would be

Insights From the Experts

"The primary finding is this: student time spent engaged in relevant content appears to be an essential variable for which there is no substitute .... Teachers who make a difference in students' achievement are those who put students into contact with curriculum materials and find ways to keep them in contact" (Rosenshine & Berliner, 1978).

targeted as an objective for his participation in the foods and nutrition class. A second, related objective focused on his use of these words in completing simple recipes at home to prepare his own lunches on the weekends.

Jacob is supported in the foods class by a special education paraprofessional who is available to work with the teacher to implement modifications and provide assistance to Jacob as necessary to complete class activities. Embedded instructional trials were provided to him through natural opportunities during the instruction provided by his general education teacher. Supplemental instructional trials were presented between class activities and during the natural breaks in class activities. During each class period the paraprofessional presented Jacob with a combination of (a) EI trials designed to systematically promote his acquisition of the skill, and (b) naturalistic trials within activities developed by the general education teacher to support the generalization of the skill to new materials and activities.

Lisa

Lisa is an 8-year-old student in the second grade diagnosed with autism spectrum disorder. Although Lisa had been given the WISC-III, a valid IQ score could not be established. Lisa was described by her teachers as very pleasant but passive. For example, she would comply with verbal requests (when paired with gestures), but she did not initiate communication bids even when she needed something. She interacted minimally with peers and only slightly more with specific adults. Lisa demonstrated some verbal imitation (i.e., repeats single words) but did not use words to express her wants and needs. She also had an electronic communication device, but did not use it to communicate with others in the environment. She received occupational therapy services weekly and demonstrated some motor imitation. Lisa often had to be redirected to instructional tasks and needed high rates of reinforcement to remain on task. She participated in the general education class during opening activities and language arts in the morning, and science and fine arts in the afternoon. Lisa was supported in the class by a special education paraprofessional who provided her with the response prompts, error corrections, and social reinforcement as necessary to complete class activities.

Lisa's IEP team consisted of her parents, special education teacher, general education teacher, speech and language pathologist, and occupational therapist. The team decided to make communication a primary focus of her IEP. In the past, Lisa's parents and teachers had tried to teach her to communicate using single words, manual signs, and a picture exchange communication system. Although Lisa would imitate some words and signs, she did not use any of these methods to spontaneously communicate at home or at school. The team decided to try an electronic communication device with vocal output. A decision was also made to focus communication on specific things that might be important to Lisa. One of the objectives included in her IEP targeted her use of the communication device to request help or assistance when she needed help on a difficult task, or when unanticipated situations arose.

EI trials were provided by the paraprofessional assigned to support her in the general education class. EI trials on the use of her communication device were distributed throughout the day to help promote the generalized use of her device. The paraprofessional was trained to take advantage of all natural opportunities for Lisa to use her communication device. For example, when she needed assistance to complete a task the paraprofessional would provide an EI trial. However, to ensure that she had a sufficient number of opportunities to learn to use her device, the teacher and the paraprofessional would engineer situations throughout the day to provide supplemental EI trials, such as asking Lisa to complete an assignment for which she did not have all the necessary materials.

Summary

Implementing EI requires a four-step process. In the first step, the teacher *prepares for instruction* by specifying goals, collecting baseline data, and developing a trial distribution schedule. In the second step, the teacher *designs an EI program* by formulating a teaching plan and establishing data collection procedures. In the third step the teacher *implements the EI program*, training instructors, monitoring program fidelity, and tracking the number of trials. Last, the teacher *supports efficient student learning* by trouble-shooting performance problems and revising the teaching plan as appropriate. Two case studies illustrate these four steps.

The following chapters are designed to illustrate how EI can be implemented with students with developmental disabilities in general education classes. Each chapter includes one or more forms developed to assist teachers to design and implement EI. Blanks of these forms are presented in the Appendix.

Preparing for Instruction

The development and implementation of effective EI requires teachers to complete several preparatory activities. These include (a) develop specific instructional goals and objectives for the student's participation in the general education class, (b) conduct baseline probes to assess the student's current performance of the target skills, and (c) develop a trial distribution schedule that allows teachers to target when instructional trials will be presented to the student.

Develop Specific Instructional Goals and Objectives

The first step in any good educational program is to develop instructional goals and objectives that explicitly define the expected outcomes for the student. In inclusive educational programs, this means that the student's IEP must include goals and objectives that clearly define what they will learn in the general education class. If the expected educational outcomes for the student are not clearly defined, it is possible for the student to be physically present in the classroom while functionally excluded from meaningful instruction (Schuster et al., 2001).

During the IEP process, the members of the team must clearly identify what the student will learn in the general education class. Some of these goals and objectives may focus on the student's acquisition of skills included in the typical general education curriculum. These objectives can be designed to focus on a subset of skills that are appropriate for the student, and target responses and evaluation procedures that will accommodate the student's unique education needs (Janey & Snell, 2000). For example, in Jacob's case his IEP team identified a goal of learning to read words and symbols from the general foods and nutrition curriculum that could be incorporated into recipes that he would use at home.

In other cases, goals and objectives may focus on the student's unique educational needs distinct from those in the typical general education curriculum. For example, Lisa's IEP team decided that she should learn how to request assistance from peers, staff, and teachers when she encountered a difficult task during class routines and activities. Although this skill is not in the general education curriculum, the ability to request help from others would improve her ability to function successfully in the general education class and other settings. By including both types of goals and objectives in the IEP, the student can be provided an educational program that will meet unique needs and improve the performance in school, home, and community settings.

Insights From the Experts

Villa and Thousand (2000) suggests that collaborative teaming is a process that requires team members to: "share knowledge and skills to generate new and novel methods for individualizing learning, without the need for dual systems of general and special education" (p. 255).

The development of meaningful goals and objectives for general education classes requires that students, parents, staff, and teachers collaborate to develop, implement, and evaluate the IEP. The premise of professionals working together to develop a student's IEP has been an essential principle of the Individuals With Disabilities Education Act (IDEA) since it was enacted. A substantial amount of literature suggests that developing and implementing IEPs that effectively support students' inclusion in general education classes requires a collaborative teaming process (Giangreco, Dennis, Cloninger, Edelman, & Schattman, 1993; Hunt, Doering, Hirose-Hatae, Maier, & Goetz, 2001; Hunt, Soto, Maier, & Doering, 2003; Salisbury, Evans, & Palombaro, 1997; York-Barr, Schultz, Doyle, Kronberg, & Crossett, 1996).

Hunt et al. (2003) describes a process for developing Unified Plans of Support (UPS). The focus of this process is to ensure that the educational plans for students identify meaningful learning outcomes that are consistent with the general education curriculum, and with the routines and activities of the general education class. However, the UPS process goes beyond simply identifying meaningful learning outcomes to include the development of the specific supports necessary to ensure that the IEP is implemented successfully. The UPS process is based on four key steps.

1. The team identifies the learning and social profile of each student.

2. Based on the profile, the team then brainstorms curricular, instructional, and social support strategies that will allow the student to successfully participate in each domain of the general education curriculum.

3. Once each support strategy is identified, a team member is assigned responsibility for ensuring that the strategy is put into place, and to coordinate the activities of other team members in implementing the strategy.

4. The team then develops and implements a system of accountability to evaluate the effectiveness of the UPS in meeting student needs. This involves regular team meetings to allow the team members to analyze the impact of each strategy and refine the UPS.

Within such a teaming process, EI would be considered one of many potential instructional strategies for supporting effective student learning. As indicated by the UPS process, the responsibility for designing and implementing EI would be assigned to one team member. Typically, this would be the student's special education teacher, who would collaborate with the general education teacher, paraprofessionals, peers, and other staff members to ensure that the EI program was being implemented successfully. Finally, the team would regularly review the effectiveness of the EI teaching plan and refine it as necessary to ensure student success.

Conduct a Baseline Probe

Prior to the development of the EI program, the teacher should conduct a baseline probe. The probe has three purposes. First, the probe should determine the student's level of performance before EI begins. This information allows the team to assess the overall effectiveness of the EI program in producing student learning. Obviously, in teaching new skills, student performance of the target skill is expected to improve across instructional sessions. The second purpose of this probe is to identify how much (if any) of the targeted skill the student can already perform correctly and independently. Finally, the probe should be structured to identify the type of assistance that will be necessary to allow the student consistently to complete the target skill correctly. This information will be used to design the assistance strategies for the student.

Assess the Student's Performance

The first purpose of the baseline probe is to determine how much of the skill the student can already do and what he still needs to learn. For example, in Jacob's case, the baseline probe focused on whether he could read any of the cooking words and measurement symbols that had been selected for instruction. Figure 3-1 presents an illustrative Baseline Probe Form for Jacob.

In the first column, the teacher listed the words and symbols selected for EI. The teacher assessed Jacob's performance by presenting a flash card with the word or symbol printed on it and presenting the cue "What does this say?" She coded Jacob's responses either correct with a "+" or incorrect with an "0" in the second column.

Baseline data should be collected across several sessions in order to establish a stable pattern of performance and to ensure that the data are reliable. The data in Jacob's example showed that he was able to correctly read three words and symbols (e.g., "Pan," "Ladle," and "C") across three baseline probe sessions. These three skills will be eliminated from the list of targeted skills when his teacher develops the EI teaching plan.

Lisa's teacher and the paraprofessional used the same procedures to establish her baseline performance (Figure 3-2). The data showed that she did not initiate pressing the "Help" icon during any of the probe trials. Based on the probes, the teacher and the paraprofessional decided that all of the situations assessed during the probe should be included in the EI teaching plan.

Identify the Level of Assistance

Another critical element of the baseline probe is to determine the amount of assistance that the student requires to consistently complete the correct response during instruction. This can be accomplished by implementing a prompting system known as the System of Least Prompts (SLP) each time the student makes an error during the probe.

Figure 3-1

Illustrative Baseline Probe Form for Jacob

Student: Jacob   **Teacher: Ms. Smith**
Instructional Cue: "What does this say?"

Example	1/5		1/6		1/7	
	+/0	Prompt	+/0	Prompt	+/0	Prompt
Pan	+		+		+	
Casserole	0	Model	0	Model	0	Model
Colander	0	Model	0	Model	0	Model
Ladle	+		+		+	
Spoon	0	Model	0	Model	0	Model
Tongs	0	Model	0	Model	0	Model
Spatula	0	Model	0	Model	0	Model
Whisk	0	Model	0	Model	0	Model
Strainer	0	Model	0	Model	0	Model
T	0	Model	0	Model	0	Model
T	0	Model	0	Model	0	Model
C	+		+		+	
Qt	0	Model	0	Model	0	Model
Oz	0	Model	0	Model	0	Model
Lb	0	Model	0	Model	0	Model
% Correct	20%		20%		20%	

Notes. V = Verbal; M = Model; G = Gesture/Point; P = Prime; F = Full Physical.

Figure 3-2

Illustrative Baseline Probe Form for Lisa

Student: Lisa   **Teacher: Mrs. Wright**

Instructional Cue: "What do you want?"

Example	10/16		10/17		10/18	
	+/0	Prompt	+/0	Prompt	+/0	Prompt
Difficult discrimination	0	G	0	F	0	G
Difficult motor response	0	G	0	F	0	F
Incorrect materials	0	V	0	G	0	V
Unclear directions or instructions	0	V	0	V	0	V
% Correct	0		0		0	

Notes. V = Verbal; M = Model; G = Gesture/Point; P = Prime; F = Full Physical.

(Additional information on response prompting and fading procedures will be provided in the next chapter.)

In the SLP, the teacher provides increasing amounts of assistance to the student until he makes the correct response. The type of prompts provided to the student is based on the skill that is being taught and range from verbal directions to hand-over-hand physical assistance. Once the teacher identifies the prompt that consistently results in the correct response, it is recorded on the Baseline Probe Form.

For example, Jacob did not respond when his teacher presented the flash card with the word "casserole" printed on it. After presenting the instructional cue ("What does this say?"), she waited for several seconds and then said "Casserole," and Jacob repeated the word. If Jacob had not imitated her model, she would have provided a more explicit verbal prompt to Jacob to say the word after she did (i.e., "Jacob, this word says 'casserole'. Say 'Casserole.'"). After the probe trial, his teacher then entered the word "model" in the third column of the form to record the level of assistance he needed to read the word correctly. She used this information later to design the assistance strategy for his EI program.

In contrast, Lisa required a number of different prompts to press the "help" icon on her communication device ranging from verbal prompts to full physical. This information will need to be taken into consideration in selecting the type of response prompting and fading procedure to be used with Lisa, and in designing the procedure so that it ensures her correct responding during instruction.

Develop a Trial Distribution Schedule

A key difference between EI and traditional instructional approaches is that in EI the instructional trials are distributed within and/or across classroom activities.

There are three critical steps in developing an effective EI schedule.

Step 1: Identify the Number of Instructional Trials

The rate at which students learn new skills is directly linked to the number of instructional trials they receive (Brophy & Good, 1986; Greenwood, Delquadri, & Hall, 1984; Reynolds, 1991; Rosenshine & Stevens, 1986). Put simply, the more opportunities students have to practice a skill, the faster they will learn it. The number of instructional trials a student requires is a professionally subjective judgment based on (a) the student's functioning level, (b) the complexity of the skill being taught, and (c) the structure of the activities and routines of the general education class. The best measure of how many trials the student will need is the student's previous learning history with similar skills and in similar situations. In general it

---

is probably better to overestimate the number of trials that the student will need rather than underestimate.

In Jacob's case, his teacher decided that he should receive at least five presentations of each word or symbol name each day. This meant that she would need to identify at least five situations during the foods class when the paraprofessional could present the words or symbols without disrupting the class or interfering with Jacob's involvement in other class activities.

Step 2: Determine if Trials Should be Distributed Within or Across Instructional Activities

Once the number of instructional trials necessary to promote learning is identified, the teacher must decide whether the trials will be presented within a single class period or across class periods throughout the school day. For example, teaching Jacob to read vocabulary words in the foods class would most logically be done within the regularly scheduled foods class period.

However, in other cases skills might be taught more effectively throughout the day. In teaching Lisa to request assistance, it would be more effective to distribute instructional trials through out the day because she will need to use this skill across areas of the curriculum and in different activities.

Step 3: Estimate the Frequency of Teaching Opportunities

The estimation of teaching opportunities should include both natural and supplemental embedded instruction trials. Natural embedded instruction trials are not directly controlled by the teacher, and present themselves periodically to the student within the normal flow of instructional activities presented by the general education teacher. Natural instructional trials have both advantages and disadvantages. A significant advantage is that they create opportunities for the student to respond to typical materials and in typical situations. This increases the likelihood that the student will develop a generalized skill that he or she can use in new contexts and situations.

For example, natural embedded instruction trails could occur as a result of students interacting with materials. In Jacob's foods class, it is likely that there would be opportunities for him to read the targeted words and symbols when they were presented on worksheets or the textbook. Natural instructional trials also can be linked to specific instructional activities presented by the teacher. In Jacob's case there would be opportunities for him to read the target words and symbols while completing a recipe during a cooking lab or while putting cooking utensils away following a teacher demonstration.

The disadvantage of natural instructional trials is that the teacher may not always be able to predict when these instructional trials will occur. This may reduce the potential effectiveness of instruction because the teacher may not be able to provide a consistent number of trials to the student.

To ensure that the instruction will be successful, the teacher can provide supplemental embedded instruction trials to the student. Supplemental trials are directly controlled by the individual implementing the program. They are planned teaching opportunities that occur at specific times within or across class periods. In many respects, supplemental embedded instructional trails look and feel much like the discrete trials presented to students during traditional one-to-one or small-group instruction formats. Previous research suggests that there are several common situations in general education classes in which supplemental trials can be presented (Johnson et al., 2004; Johnson & McDonnell, 2004; McDonnell et al., 2002; Wolery et al., 1997).

One possibility uses the transitions between instructional activities. For example, an instructional trial could be presented to a student as the class moves from a group instructional activity to independent seat work. Another common opportunity is natural breaks in activities. In the foods class, for example, there may be some "down time" when students are waiting for food to come out of the oven during the cooking lab. Finally, EI might be provided when students are working independently at their desks.

Figure 3-3 presents a planning form that teachers can use to determine the number of teaching opportunities that are available to teach a skill to a student. The first step is to list the potential natural and supplemental teaching opportunities on the form in the second column. Once the teaching opportunities have been identified, the teacher should list the classes, activities, or routines in which the skill will be taught at the top of the form. The form allows teachers to enter up to five different settings or contexts. Next, the teacher should develop an estimate of the frequency of teaching opportunities that will occur in each class period or activity. Once this information is entered, the teacher can calculate the total number of instructional opportunities that will be available to teach the skill to the student each day.

Figure 3-3

Trial Distribution Planning Form for Jacob

Student: Jacob							Teacher: Mrs. Smith
Potential Teaching Opportunities		Class/Activity/Routine					Total Opportunities
		Foods Class					
Natural Instructional Trials	Vocabulary worksheets	1-3					1-3
	Lab planner	1-3					1-3
	Recipes	1					1
	Text	1-5					1-5
Supplemental Instructional Trials	Activity transitions (Opening to lecture; lecture to individual or group activities; going to lab)	3					3
	Natural breaks in activities (lab)	1-3					1-3
	Management tasks (Roll; distribution of graded assignments)	1-2					1-2
	Independent work	3-6					3-6
Potential Opportunities		12-25					12-25

Figure 3-4

Trial Distribution Planning Form for Lisa

Student: Lisa		Class/Activity/Routine					Teacher: Mrs. Wright
Potential Teaching Opportunities		Opening	Language Arts	Science	Fine Arts		Total Opportunities
Natural Instructional Trials	Text	1	1	1	0		3
	Worksheets	1	1	1	0		3
	Collaborative group activities and projects	1	1	1	1		4
	Large group discussions	1	1	1	1		4
Supplemental Instructional Trials	Activity transitions (Opening to lecture; lecture to individual or group activities; going to lab)	1	1	1	1		4
	Natural breaks in activities (lab)	1	1	1	1		4
	Management tasks (Roll; distribution of graded assignments)	1	1	1	1		4
	Independent work	1-2	1-2	1-2	0		4-8
Potential Opportunities		8-10	8-10	8-10	4		28-34

Jacob's teacher focused her analysis on both the natural and supplemental instruction trials that would typically be available during the foods class (Figure 3-3). In completing the form, she first estimated the number of natural EI trials that might be available during a class period. These estimates were based on her discussions with the general education teacher and her previous observations of the class. Next, she estimated the frequency of the potential supplemental embedded instruction trials. Her analysis suggested that typically there would be an opportunity to present between 12 and 25 natural and supplemental instruction trials to Jacob each day. Based on this, she concluded that EI could be used to effectively teach Jacob to read the words and symbols without providing him with additional one-to-one or small-group instruction.

Lisa's teacher's concluded that natural opportunities for requesting help in the second grade class would occur at a relatively low rate during the day, based on her discussion with her general education teacher and her observations of the classroom (Figure 3-4). It became clear that supplemental instructional trials would need to be engineered to provide more opportunities for Lisa to learn when to request help. The teacher identified times during the typical routines and activities of the class in which these trials could be presented without disrupting the other students and the general education teacher.

Summary

In preparing to implement EI, the student's IEP team must work together to identify meaningful learning goals and objectives for their participation in the general education class. Once EI has been selected as an instructional strategy, the teacher should conduct a baseline probe in order to establish the student's entry level of performance on the target skills. The baseline probe also provides important information to the teacher about the examples and response prompts that should be included in the teaching plan. Finally, the teacher should identify natural and supplemental embedded instructional trials within the on-going classroom routines and activities to promote efficient learning.

Designing an Embedded Instruction Program

The basic elements of an EI program are similar to those used in traditional special education classes. Before instruction begins, the teacher should prepare a teaching plan and develop data collection procedures to allow ongoing assessment of the student's performance.

Write a Teaching Plan

Figures 4-1 and 4-2 present a form that teachers can use to write an EI Teaching Plan. To begin the process, the teacher should enter the instructional objective in the first row of the form, and enter the natural and supplemental teaching opportunities listed on the Trial Distribution Form in the second row of the form. This information will serve as a reminder to the individual implementing the program about the expected outcomes of EI and when instructional trials may be delivered to the student. The teacher will then complete additional steps to write an effective teaching plan: (a) select instructional examples and (b) develop teaching materials, (c) sequence instructional examples, (d) develop assistance strategies, and (e) develop reinforcement and (f) error correction procedures.

Select Instructional Examples and Develop Teaching Materials to Promote Generalization

Research studies on generalization consistently have concluded that many students with developmental disabilities have difficulty generalizing skills learned in one context or setting to new contexts or settings (Horner, McDonnell, & Bellamy, 1986; Rosenthal-Malek & Bloom, 1998). For example, a student might use signs to request desired items at school with his teacher but not be able to use the signs at home with his parents. Another student may learn to use one type of calculator to complete single digit addition problems but not be able to do the same problems with a different calculator. Effectively addressing this problem requires that the teacher develop a teaching plan designed to promote generalized responding from the very beginning. This is accomplished by identifying all of the situations and

---

Figure 4-1

Embedded Instruction Teaching Plan for Jacob

Student: Jacob

Instructional Objective: During his foods and nutrition class, Jacob will read cooking and measurement sight words with 80% accuracy on two consecutive probe sessions.

Naturalistic instruction opportunities:	Supplemental instruction opportunities:
Vocabulary worksheets Lab planner Recipes Text	Transitions to lecture, activities, labs Breaks during lab Roll Distribution of graded assignments

Presentation sequence:

Assistance strategy:

Reinforcement procedures:

Error correction procedures:

Figure 4-2

Embedded Instruction Teaching Plan for Lisa

Student: Lisa
Instructional Objective: In her second grade class and when presented with a difficult task or an unexpected need, Lisa will request assistance from teachers, staff, or peers without assistance on five consecutive probe sessions.

Natural instruction opportunities:	**Supplemental instruction opportunities:**
Text Worksheets Collaborative group activities/ projects Large group discussions	Transitions Natural breaks Management tasks Independent seat work

Presentation sequence:
Assistance strategy:
Reinforcement procedures:
Error correction procedures:

settings across which the student must use the skill, and then developing instructional examples and materials that systematically present the necessary situational variations to the student across trials and sessions. To accomplish this, the teacher should complete the following three activities.

Identify the performance contexts in which the student will use the skill. The first thing the teacher must do is to decide where and when the student will be required to use the skill. For example, in Jacob's case, he should be able to read the target words and symbols during instructional activities in his foods class and when completing recipes at home. For Lisa, the variation in requesting help is related more to the specific situations in which she should ask for assistance rather than settings. This information will help the teacher identify the range of situations that the student will encounter in using the skill from day-to-day, and how his or her use of the skill will change based on this variation.

Identify how the performance contexts are different from each other. Once the range of performance contexts have been identified, the teacher should identify the ways that the various contexts differ from each other. In reading the target words and symbols, one of the biggest differences is the physical characteristics of the words that are presented to Jacob. For instance, the size of the letters, the font, and the color of the letters in the word "whisk" will vary based on whether he is reading it out of the textbook, from a worksheet developed by the teacher, or as part of a recipe from a cookbook. For Lisa, determining when to request help would vary significantly across different situations and would require her to recognize that she either did not know what to do or that she did not have the necessary materials to complete the task. This information helps the teacher determine the kinds of supplemental instructional examples that should be presented to the student across teaching sessions and how the instructional materials will need to be designed to ensure that the student develops a generalized response.

Develop instructional examples and materials that expose students to the variation in the performance contexts. Teaching generalized responses requires the teacher to present examples and materials to the student that require him or her to respond correctly across the variation found in the intended performance contexts. In EI programs, this can be accomplished by designing teaching examples and materials that presents this variation across EI trials. It is also accomplished by identifying opportunities within the ongoing activities of the general education class to present naturalistic instruction trials. In Jacob's case, the teacher would develop teaching materials for embedded instruction trials that varied the physical characteristics of the target words and symbols. This could be accomplished by developing a set of flash cards that varied the size, font, and color of each of the words (e.g., whisk, whisk, whisk). Different flash cards of each word would be presented to Jacob across EI trials within a class period. Ideally, Jacob would never see the same flashcard twice in a class period. For Lisa, this could be accomplished by presenting different situations (e.g., pointing to the correct word during language arts, using scissors during fine arts) within and across class periods. The teacher would need to engineer different examples within each "help" category (e.g., difficult discriminations, difficult motor responses) each day. The goal would be to present as many different examples within each "help" category as possible across the week.

In addition, the development of generalized responses is also promoted by taking advantage of the natural teaching opportunities that are presented during the ongoing activities of the class. For example, this could be accomplished by asking Jacob to read the word "whisk" each time it is presented on a worksheet, in the textbook, in a recipe, and so on. The physical characteristics of the word "whisk," as well as whether it is presented in isolation, in a sentence, or as label for a picture, are likely to vary substantially across each of these contexts. For Lisa, her paraprofessional would look for situations in which she was not successfully completing a task assigned to other students in the class, and prompt her to ask for help from her peers or teacher.

Develop a Presentation Sequence

Developing an effective example presentation sequence requires the teacher to determine how many instructional examples should be presented to the student at one time. The teacher then should arrange the sequence so examples can be cumulatively introduced to the student across instructional sessions.

A key decision in developing a teaching plan is deciding how many instructional examples can be introduced to the student at *one time*. Systematically controlling the introduction and presentation of examples can significantly increase the efficiency of instruction and reduce the number of errors that the student makes while learning the skill. For example, it would probably be too difficult for Jacob to learn all of the words and symbols simultaneously. Consequently, his teacher needs to divide the complete list of targeted words into smaller teaching sets, and introduce them to him in a way that allows him to retain the skill across time. The baseline probe indicated that he could only read 3 of the 15 words and symbols that were selected for instruction. Consequently, his teacher decided that she would break the remaining 12 words into 3 teaching sets, each consisting of 4 words or symbols.

By dividing examples into sets, teachers can both control the difficulty of the instructional task for the student and increase the speed at which he learns the skill. The decision about how many examples can be presented to a student should be based on several factors.

- *The student's previous learning history.* A fundamental principle of effective instruction is that the strategies are tailored to a student's specific needs. The best basis on which to make a decision about how many examples to include in a teaching set is the student's previous performance in other instructional programs.

- *The complexity or difficulty of the skill.* The size of the teaching set should also be based on the complexity or difficulty of the skill being taught. The goal is to present the maximum number of examples that allow the student to experience success. As a result, more complex or difficult skills will probably require the teacher to develop smaller teaching sets.

- *The nature of the teaching opportunities.* Another consideration involves the characteristics of the teaching opportunities available within class periods or activities. For example, the teacher might have less time to present instructional examples to the student during transitions between instructional activities (i.e., between small group discussion and starting work on a worksheet) in the foods class than during independent work at the lab station.

Sequencing teaching examples. An especially effective strategy for introducing a large number of teaching examples to students is called cumulative sequencing. In this strategy, the first teaching example is introduced and taught to criterion. Then, the second example is introduced and taught to criterion. In the third step of the sequence, the student is required to accurately respond to both examples when presented randomly. Each subsequent teaching example initially is taught by itself. Then all of the previously taught examples are mixed together and presented randomly to the student. This strategy allows the teacher to cumulatively increase the number of examples the student completes, and provides the student with regular opportunities to review previously taught examples.

This strategy can be applied to individual teaching examples, or as in Jacob's case, to sets of examples. Figure 4-3 presents the sequence developed by his teacher. In the first step of the sequence, the first 4 vocabulary words are introduced to Jacob and instruction is provided until he can read the words at the expected criterion. Next, the teacher introduces the second set of words and teaches it to criterion. In the third step of the sequence, the teacher will ask Jacob to read all of the words in the first two sets when they are presented randomly during the class session. This ensures that Jacob is not mixing up words that are similar in structure (i.e., "spatula" and "spoon") and that he has not forgotten the first 4 words that were taught. In the third step of the sequence, the next set of words is taught. Finally, he is required to read all 12 words and symbols when presented in random order through out the class session.

Figure 4-3

Presentation Sequence for Jacob

Student: Jacob
Instructional Objective: During his foods and nutrition class, Jacob will read cooking and measurement sight words with 80% accuracy on two consecutive probe sessions.

Naturalistic instruction opportunities	Supplemental instruction opportunities:
Vocabulary worksheets Lab planner Recipes Text	Transitions to lecture; activities, labs Breaks during lab Roll Distribution of graded assignments

Presentation sequence:
1. Casserole, tongs, spatula, T   4. Strainer, t, oz, lb 2. Colander, spoon, whisk, qt   5. All examples. 3. Sets 1 and 2 together
Assistance strategy:
Reinforcement procedures:
Error correction procedures:

Lisa's teacher decided to use a different approach to teach her to request help (Figure 4-4). Instead of cumulatively introducing the "help" categories to her, the teacher decided to randomly present different examples within each category throughout the day. This procedure is called concurrent presentation. The teacher selected this procedure because (a) it would be difficult, if not impossible, to present multiple embedded instruction trials at one time to Lisa; and (b) there was only one possible response that Lisa could make (i.e., press the help icon) to each example that was presented. In these cases, the random presentation of examples allows the student to be exposed to the full range of variation associated with the target skill and to learn a generalized response.

Develop an Assistance Strategy

Most students with developmental disabilities will need assistance from a teacher to learn new skills. A variety of strategies can be used, including providing physical assistance (e.g., hand-over-hand to help the student write the letters of his first name), picture prompts (e.g., providing the student with a printed card of his name so that he can copy his name onto his worksheet), modeling (e.g., demonstrating how the letters of his first name are made), and verbal directions (e.g., telling the student to print his first name in the upper right hand corner). After the student begins to acquire the skill, the teacher should begin to fade out the assistance strategies so that the student can perform the skill without assistance. Research has validated a number of fading strategies with students with developmental disabilities (Wolery et al., 1992). They include the system of most prompts, time delay, graduated guidance, and the system of least prompts. While all of these strategies can be used to teach new skills, we recommend that teachers use a constant-time delay strategy in for most students and skills. A number of studies have shown that constant-time delay those in EI programs (Johnson & McDonnell, 2004; McDonnell, Johnson, Polychronis, & Riesen, 2002; Riesen, McDonnell, Johnson, Polychronis, & Jameson, 2003). In addition, teachers and paraprofessionals participating in these studies have reported that constant time delay is a simple and easy strategy to implement within the ongoing routines and activities of general education classes.

Using the constant time-delay procedure, an instructional trial begins with the teacher presenting the example and an instructional cue that tells the student what he is expected to do. Then the teacher provides assistance or a controlling prompt to ensure that the student correctly completes the expected response. In the first step of constant time delay, the teacher presents the controlling prompt to the student immediately following the example and the instructional cue. This step is referred to as the 0-second delay step. The teacher continues to implement this

Figure 4-4

Presentation Sequence for Lisa

Student: Lisa
Instructional Objective: In her second grade class and when presented with a difficult task or an unexpected need, Lisa will request assistance from teachers, staff, or peers without assistance on five consecutive probe sessions.

Natural instruction opportunities:
    Text
    Worksheets
    Collaborative group activities/
    projects
    Large group discussions
	Supplemental instruction opportunities:
	    Transitions
	    Natural breaks
	    Management tasks
	    Independent seat work

Presentation Sequence:
 	
Random presentation of the following situations:
   1. **Difficult discrimination (e.g., pointing to the correct object).**
   2. **Difficult motor response (e.g., opening the crayon box, cutting with sessions).**
   3. **Not having correct materials (e.g., not having a pencil).**
   4. **Unclear directions/instructions. (e.g., give materials without verbal prompts).**

Assistance Strategy:
Reinforcement Procedures:
Error Correction Procedures:

is an effective strategy for students with developmental disabilities, including step until the student is responding reliably to the prompt. In the second step, the teacher delays the presentation of the controlling prompt for a fixed amount of time. Typically this delay period is several seconds. Delaying the controlling prompt provides the student an opportunity to respond correctly without help or additional information. If the student doesn't correctly complete the response during the delay period, then the teacher provides the controlling prompt to the student.

Figure 4-5 presents the constant time-delay procedure developed by Jacob's teacher. In the first step (Roman numeral I), each instructional trial begins with the teacher presenting a flash card (i.e., the symbol "t" for "teaspoon") and providing the instructional cue, "What does this say?" The teacher immediately provides the controlling prompt (i.e., the teacher says "Teaspoon"). Instruction continues at this step until Jacob reliably responds correctly for each word in the teaching set.

Box 4-1: Common Response Prompting and Fading Procedures

Constant Time Delay - Prompts are faded by inserting a fixed amount of time between the instructional cue and the controlling prompt.

Progressive Time Delay - Prompts are faded by gradually increasing the amount of time between the instructional cue and the controlling prompt.

System of Most Prompts - The amount of assistance provided to the student prior to the target response is gradually reduced across instructional trials or sessions.

System of Least Prompts - Following an error, the amount of assistance provided to the student is gradually increased until he completes the target response.

At this point, the teacher moves to the second step of the procedure. In this step (Roman numeral II), the teacher begins each trial by presenting a flash card (the symbol "t") and the instructional cue ("What does this say?"). However, instead of providing the controlling prompt immediately, she delays the modeling prompt for three seconds. If Jacob does not correctly read the word or symbol during the three second delay period, she presents the controlling prompt by saying "teaspoon."

Successfully implementing constant time-delay within an EI program requires teachers to identify a cue that will tell the student what he is expected to do, identify the controlling prompt, and determine how long the delay period should be *Identifying an instructional cue.* Often the instructional cue can be a verbal direction that tells the student that it is time to respond and what he is to do. However, many types of assistance could be used as an instructional cue. The cue should be selected based on student preference, the nature of the skill, and the expected response.

Figure 4-5

Assistance Strategy for Jacob

Student: Jacob
Instructional Objective: During his foods and nutrition class, Jacob will read cooking and measurement sight words with 80% accuracy on two consecutive probe sessions.

Embedded instruction opportunities:	Naturalistic instruction opportunities:
Transitions to lecture; activities, labs Breaks during lab Roll Distribution of graded assignments	Vocabulary worksheets Lab planner Recipes Text

Presentation Sequence:
1. Casserole, Tongs, Spatula, T   4. Strainer, t, oz, lb 2. Colander, Spoon, Whisk, qt   5. All examples. 3. Sets 1 and 2 together
Assistance Strategy: **I. "What does this say?" present model immediately.** **II. "What does this say?" delay model for 3 seconds.**
Reinforcement Procedures:
Error Correction Procedures:

Identify the controlling prompt. Research suggests that teachers should attempt to minimize the number of errors that students make when they are first learning a new skill (Westling & Fox, 2004; Wolery et al., 1992). This minimizes the need for a student to subsequently "unlearn" the mistake. Consequently, the teacher should use controlling prompts that are most likely to result in the student making the correct response during each instructional trial. This information is obtained during the baseline probe. During the probe, the teacher should have identified the type and amount of assistance that would be necessary for the student to correctly complete the desired response. This assistance strategy is then used as the controlling prompt in both steps of the constant-time delay procedure.

Determining the length of the delay period. There are no validated rules for selecting the length for the delay period in a constant time delay-procedure. The delay periods in research studies examining constant time-delay have varied widely (Wolery et al., 1992). A teacher's decision about the length of the delay period will always be somewhat subjective. One approach to help make this process more systematic is to estimate how quickly students without disabilities would typically respond in similar situations. Once this has been established, the teacher can adjust the delay period to accommodate the unique characteristics and needs of the student. Three second to 10 second delays are typical.

Other response prompting and fading procedures. Certain response prompting strategies may be more effective for certain tasks or for certain students. As indicated in Chapter 1, research has demonstrated that simultaneous prompting, the system of least prompts, and the system of most prompts can be used effectively in embedded instruction. For example, in Lisa's case, her teacher previously had used constant time-delay to teach several discrete skills with limited success. However, the system of least prompts had been effective in teaching her a variety of skills. Based on Lisa's previous learning history her teacher decided to use the system of least prompts to teach her to request help. Figure 4-6 illustrates how this system was entered on the teaching plan form.

Develop Reinforcement and Error Correction Procedures

The last two components of the teaching plan are the reinforcement and error correction procedures. Students can make three possible responses during an instructional trial when using a constant time-delay procedure. These include (a) correct responses that are not prompted by the teacher, (b) correct responses that are prompted by the teacher, and (c) incorrect responses (including no response). Teachers should develop specific consequence procedures to address each of these responses (Wolery et al., 1992). Once the teacher has developed procedures for each of these three possible responses, that information should be entered on the Teaching Plan (Figure 4-7).

Figure 4-6

Assistance Strategies for Lisa

Student: Lisa
Instructional Objective: In her second grade class and when presented with a difficult task or an unexpected need, Lisa will request assistance from teachers, staff, or peers without assistance on five consecutive probe sessions.

Natural instruction opportunities: 　Text 　Worksheets 　Collaborative group activities/projects 　Large group discussions	Supplemental instruction opportunities: 　Transitions 　Natural Breaks 　Management Tasks 　Independent Seat Work

Presentation Sequence: Random presentation of the following situations: 　1.　Difficult discrimination (e.g., pointing to the correct object). 　2.　Difficult motor response (e.g., opening the crayon box, cutting with sessions). 　3.　Not having correct materials (e.g., not having a pencil). 　4.　Unclear directions/instructions. (e.g., give materials without verbal prompts).
Assistance Strategy – System of Least Prompts: 　**1.　Situation presented wait 3 seconds.** 　**2.　Say "What do you want?" and point to communicator – wait 3 seconds.** 　**3.　Say "What do you want?" and point to the help icon – wait 3 seconds.** 　**4.　Say "What do you want?" and provide physical assistance to touch help icon.**
Reinforcement Procedures:
Error Correction Procedures:

Figure 4-7

Reinforcement and Error Correction Procedures for Jacob

Student: Jacob
Instructional Objective: During his foods and nutrition class, Jacob will read cooking and measurement sight words with 80% accuracy on two consecutive probe sessions.

Naturalistic Instruction Opportunities	Supplemental instruction opportunities:
Vocabulary worksheets Lab planner Recipes Text	Transitions to lecture; activities, labs Breaks during lab Roll Distribution of graded assignments

Presentation Sequence:

1. Casserole, Tongs, Spatula, T
2. Colander, Spoon, Whisk, qt
3. Sets 1 and 2 together

4. Strainer, t, oz, lb
5. All examples.

Assistance Strategy:

I. "What does this say?" present model immediately.

II. "What does this say?" delay model for 3 seconds.

Reinforcement Procedures:
    Unprompted: Social praise plus "That says word/symbol name."
    Prompted: "That says word/symbol name."

Error Correction Procedures:
    Stop the trial immediately. Say "No, that's not right."
    Represent the flash card and the cue "What does this say?"
    Immediately provide a model of the work/symbol name.
    Confirm the correct response by saying "That word says word/
    symbol name."

Unprompted correct responses. An unprompted correct response means that the student makes the correct response before the teacher presents the controlling prompt. This response is exactly what the EI program is designed to establish. Consequently, the teacher should provide high levels of reinforcement for this response. For example, Jacob's teacher decided to provide descriptive social praise each time he read a word or symbol without any assistance. If he read the word before she could model it for him, she would say something like "Very good! That says word/symbol name."

Prompted correct responses. A prompted correct response means that the student makes the correct response after the controlling prompt has been presented by the teacher. In these instances, the teacher should confirm that the student made the correct response. However, the student should not be provided the same level of reinforcement as an unprompted independent correct response. This differential level of feedback is necessary to minimize the likelihood that the student will learn to wait for the teacher's prompt. For example, Jacob's teacher decided to simply say "That says (word/symbol name)" if he read the word or symbol correctly after her model.

Incorrect responses. The constant time-delay procedure is designed to minimize the number of incorrect responses that students make during instruction. (For these purposes, "no response" is considered to be an incorrect response.) Some degree of student error is unavoidable. However, research suggests that the effectiveness of instruction can be improved if student errors are systematically corrected (Barbetta, Heron, & Heward, 1993; Barbetta, Heward, Bradely, & Miller, 1994). It is recommended that teachers use a four-step process to correct student errors.

- Stop the instructional trial immediately and provide the student with feedback that he has made an incorrect response.
- Present the example and instructional cue to the student.
- Provide the student with the level of assistance necessary to ensure a correct response on the next attempt.
- Provide feedback to confirm the correct response.

This procedure is simple and can be implemented quickly with a student. It also can be adapted for a wide variety of instructional tasks and skills. The error correction procedure that Jacob's teacher plans to use with him based on this four-step procedure is presented in Figure 4-7.

Variations in reinforcement and error correction procedures. The guidelines described previously are equally applicable for reinforcing correct responses or correcting errors when using the simultaneous prompting procedure, the system of most prompts, or the system of least prompts. However, the teacher may need to be provided additional information in the teaching plan about the prompt to be used to correct an error when using the system of most prompts or the system of least prompts. Figure 4-8 illustrates the reinforcement and error correction procedures developed by Lisa's teacher for the system of least prompts.

Establish Data Collection and Summary Procedures

Research has documented that the efficiency of instruction is improved if the teacher continuously tracks the student's performance (Farlow & Snell, 1994). This information can be used to help make modifications in the teaching procedures so that they can be tailored to the student's unique needs. General guidelines for carrying out data collection and interpreting student performance data have been discussed extensively elsewhere (Farlow & Snell, 1994; Westling & Fox, 2004; Wolery, Bailey, & Sugai, 1988). Although continuous trial-by-trial data collection is a very common approach to gathering performance data with students with developmental disabilities, these procedures may be difficult to implement when instruction trials are distributed within and across activities in general education classes. Consequently, it is recommended that teachers use data collection systems that are designed to regularly probe the student's performance of the target task.

Figure 4-8

Reinforcement and Error Correction Procedures for Lisa

Student: Lisa
Instructional Objective: In her second grade class and when presented with a difficult task or an unexpected need, Lisa will request assistance from teachers, staff, or peers without assistance on five consecutive probe sessions.

Natural instruction opportunities:	Supplemental instruction opportunities:
Text Worksheets Collaborative group activities/projects Large group discussions	Transitions Natural breaks Management tasks Independent seat work

Presentation Sequence:
Random presentation of the following situations:

1. Difficult discrimination (e.g., pointing to the correct object).
2. Difficult motor response (e.g., opening the crayon box, cutting with sessions).
3. Not having correct materials (e.g., not having a pencil).
4. Unclear directions/instructions. (e.g., give materials without verbal prompts).

Assistance Strategy – System of Least Prompts:

1. Situation presented wait 3 seconds.
2. Say "What do you want?" and point to communicator – wait 3 seconds.
3. Say "What do you want?" and point to the help icon – wait 3 seconds
4. Say "What do you want?" and provide physical assistance to touch help icon.

Reinforcement Procedures:
  Unprompted: Provide descriptive social praise (e.g., "Excellent, you asked for help").
  Prompted: Provide feedback (e.g., "That's how you ask for help").

Error Correction Procedures:
  Stop the trial immediately. Say "No, you need to ask for help."
  Immediately provide the next level of prompt in the sequence.
  Confirm the correct response by saying "That's how you ask for help."

In a probe system, the teacher would probe or test the student's performance of the skill on a fixed schedule. The decision about when probes should be conducted is based on factors such as the student's needs, the complexity of the task, the student's previous learning history, and the organization of the general education class. An example of an EI Probe Sheet is presented in Figure 4-9.

In Jacob's case, his teacher decided that she should collect probe data on his performance twice a week. The probes were conducted during independent work periods scheduled by his general education teacher. On January 9th, the parapro-fessional probed Jacob on the words and symbols included in the first set. During the probe, she presented the flash cards in random order and asked "What does this say?" She did not provide a model of the word during the probe. If he read the word correctly, she entered a "+" on the probe sheet for correct responses and a "0" if he read it incorrectly (Figure 4-9).

For example, on 1/9 the data indicate that Jacob was only able to read the symbol for "tablespoon" ("T") correctly. Next, she calculated the percentage of correct responses that he made during the probe and entered these data on a graph. The graph allows her to visually analyze his performance data to determine whether he is making adequate progress toward meeting the objective (Figure 4-10). In addition, the probe sheet also allows Jacob's teacher to track his errors on specific words across probe sessions. This information can be used to change the instruc-tional procedures as necessary to provide Jacob more practice on words that are difficult for him.

The form shows that Jacob met criterion on the first teaching set on 1/18. The teacher then introduced the second teaching set for instruction. The teacher would probe Jacob's performance on the second teaching set on the same schedule. It is also recommended that previously introduced teaching examples continued to be probed to ensure that the student is maintaining their performance.

Summary

The components of a teaching plan for EI are similar to those used in most tradi-tional special education instruction approaches. As with all teaching plans, the teacher should employ evidenced-based practices tailored to the individual needs of the student and the skill being taught. The difference between EI and traditional instructional programs is that the trials are distributed during classroom activities and routines. Consequently, the teacher must identify natural and supplemental opportunities to provide instruction to the student. In addition, the teacher must ensure that the individual who is carrying out instruction can reliably identify and take advantage of these opportunities. The teacher must also monitor the student's performance in EI programs. It is recommended that regular probes of the student performance be used to accomplish this goal. The frequency of probe sessions should be tailored to the student's needs.

Figure 4-9

Illustrative Probe Sheet

Student: Jacob						Teacher: Mrs. Smith			
Example/ Item	Date								
	1/9	1/11	1/16	1/18	1/22				
Casserole	0	0	0	+	+				
Tongs	0	0	+	+	+				
Spatula	0	+	+	+	+				
T	+	+	+	+	+				
Percentage Correct	20	50	75	100	100				

Figure 4-10

Graph of Jacob's Performance During Probe Sessions

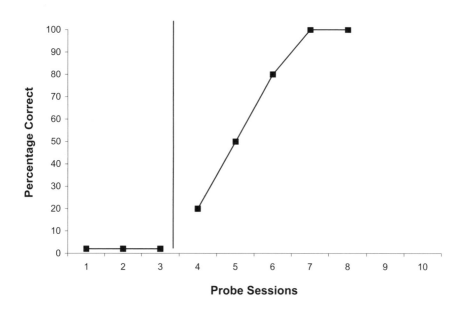

CHAPTER

5

Implementing the Embedded Instruction Program

The success of EI hinges upon consistent implementation of the teaching plan. The same instructional procedures should be implemented with both natural and supplemental embedded instruction trials. In order to achieve this outcome, the teacher must (a) train the instructors (e.g., special education paraprofessionals, student peers, etc.) to reliably implement EI; (b) monitor the fidelity of program implementation by instructors; and (c) monitor the number of natural and supplemental EI trials being presented to the student within and across instructional sessions.

Train Instructors

One of the challenges in successfully implementing EI is ensuring that the individuals carrying it out are taking advantage of all possible opportunities to present instructional trials to the student and are implementing teaching procedures consistently. Research focused on validating procedures for effectively training individuals to implement EI has increased in the last several years (Jameson et al., 2007; Johnson & McDonnell, 2004; McBride & Schwartz, 2003; VanDerheyden et al., 2005; Wolery et al., 1997). These studies have identified several procedures that can improve the quality and effectiveness of training provided to instructors. These procedures include the teacher providing (a) written materials that describe the procedures to the instructor, (b) modeling and role play prior to implementation of EI in the classroom, and (c) modeling and guided practice in implementing the procedures in the classroom.

> ### *Insights From the Experts*
>
> "There should be a match between the agreed upon paraprofessionals' roles and the skills, training, and support they have to engage in those roles…If a paraprofessional is asked to implement specialized instruction, he or she should receive specific training and support in how to implement such instruction" (Giangreco, Edelman, & Broer, 2001, p. 495).

Written Materials

Research suggests that instructors benefit from reviewing brief and clearly written materials about EI prior to implementing it with students in the classroom. In our own work, these materials typically include a description of EI and rationale for its use in the classroom, a description of how EI will be implemented with students, illustrations of when EI trials can be presented to the student, and examples of the teaching plan and data collection forms to be used by the instructor. These materials are used during the training to help communicate what is expected of the instructor and to serve as a future reference for the instructor if they have questions. An example of materials developed to train middle school peers without disabilities to implement EI is presented in Appendix B (Jameson et al., 2007).

Modeling and Role Play

Another strategy that has proven to be effective is for the teacher to model the procedures during a role play with the instructor, and then have the instructor demonstrate the procedures during role play with the teacher acting as student. During this role play, the teacher should provide the full range of possible responses that a student might make during EI, including correct responses, no responses, or incorrect responses. The teacher should provide on-going feedback to the instructor on the implementation of the procedures until a prespecified performance criterion (e.g., five consecutive trials without errors) is met.

Modeling and Guided Practice in the Classroom

Insights From the Experts

"Helping peers to support their classmates with severe disabilities consists of several steps. Peers are provided with a rationale for their involvement in delivery support to their classmates, an overview of their teachers' expectations related to this role, and information about how their classmates communicate, interact with their environment, and learn most effectively" (Carter & Kennedy, 2006, p. 285).

The final strategy is to model the implementation of EI and provide guided practice to the instructor with the student in the classroom. The teacher first demonstrates the implementation of the strategies laid out in the teaching plan. Next, the instructor implements the strategies with on-going assistance and feedback from the teacher. Finally, the instructor is asked to implement the strategies without assistance from the teacher. Modeling and guided practice continues with the instructor until he/she is able to meet a prespecified performance criterion. A reasonable criterion is 100% accuracy in implementing the teaching plan across two consecutive EI sessions.

Monitor Program Fidelity

A critical implementation issue is whether the EI teaching plan is being implemented consistently by those providing support to the student. This is important because it is impossible to assess the fundamental effectiveness of the EI program if it is not being implemented the same way across class periods, routines, or activities. Consequently, the teacher must regularly observe the individuals who are implementing the EI program in the general education class.

Figure 5-1 presents a form that teachers can use to carry out a fidelity observation. The first column includes the steps of the teaching plan designed for the student. The specific steps included in this column can be adjusted to reflect variations in response prompting and fading procedures, error correction procedures, and so on. The top row includes the student's name, the individual implementing the EI program, the step of the EI Teaching Plan being implemented, and the date of the observation. The next two rows indicate the trial number and whether the trial was a natural (N) or supplemental (S) embedded instructional trial. The teacher should try to observe as many trials as possible during the session. The frequency of fidelity observations should be adjusted based on the complexity of the skills being taught and whether the student has unique needs that may influence the efficacy of instruction (e.g., behavior problems, side effects of medications). When an instructor is first learning to implement EI, the teacher should observe more frequently. As the instructor become more proficient, the frequency of observation can be reduced to a level that accommodates the student, the skill, and the class.

Box 5-1: Recommended Fidelity Observation Schedule for New Instructors.

1. Daily until they implement the teaching plan with 100% accuracy on two consecutive observations.

2. Weekly until they implement the teaching plan with 100% accuracy on two consecutive observations. (Note: Peers should continue to be observed weekly through the program)

4. Bi-monthly until they implement the teaching plan with 100% accuracy on two consecutive observations.

4. Observe as necessary to ensure the effectiveness of EI.

To complete the form, the teacher would simply enter "+" in the box for each trial if the individual's teaching behavior was consistent with the procedures laid out in the teaching plan. The teacher would enter a "0" if the individual's behavior was inconsistent with the plan. Following the observation, the instructor's overall level of fidelity would be summarized by calculating the percentage of program steps implemented correctly.

Figure 5-1

Illustrative Program Monitoring Form

Student: Jacob			EI Program Step: II/2		
Instructor: Karen			Date: 1/17		
Program Step Trial	1	2	3	4	5
	S	N	S	S	S
1. Initiates an instructional trial at planned times or when a natural opportunity occurs.	+	+	+	+	+
2. Varies instructional materials.	+	0	+	+	+
3. Obtains student's attention.	+	+	+	+	+
4. Delivers instructional cue.	+	+	+	+	+
5. Delays controlling prompt.	+	0	+	0	+
6. Delivers controlling prompt.	+	+	+	+	+
7. Provides correct level of reinforcement (unprompted or prompted). OR Implements error correction procedure.	+	+	+	+	+
8. Records trial on tracking form.	+	+	+	+	+
Percentage Correct (Total Correct Steps/Total Steps x 100)	37/40 x 100 = 92.5%				

In the example, Jacob's teacher set up the form to reflect her expectation that Karen would vary the stimulus cards on each supplemental trial with Jacob and that she use a 3-second time-delay procedure. She also noted on the form that Karen was to implement step 2/II of the teaching plan with Jacob during the observation. This meant that Karen was supposed to present the second word set ("colander," "spoon," "whisk," "qt") using a 3 second time-delay. Karen provided Jacob with 4 supplemental trials and 1 natural trial during the class period.

The data indicate that she forgot to change the flash cards used to present the words to Jacob in one trial, and that she did not delay the controlling prompt for 3 seconds in two of the trials. Her overall level of fidelity during the class period was 92.5%. Although this is a very good level of fidelity, the fact that she did not delay the controlling prompt the appropriate amount of time during two of the trials should be addressed by the teacher. At this point, the teacher should provide Karen with feedback about the errors and remind her to be sure to delay the controlling prompt. However, if Karen made the same mistake during her next observation, there may be a need for the teacher to provide additional training on implementing the EI program.

Track the Presentation of EI and Naturalistic Trials

Figure 5-2 presents a form that is designed to allow the teacher to track the number of natural and supplemental embedded instruction trials provided to the student by the instructor. It also serves as a reminder to the instructor to make sure to provide the number of scheduled trials during each session. In setting up the form, the teacher enters the class periods and activities in which embedded instruction should be implemented with the student in the first row. The form is structured to allow the teacher to list up to five activities or routines in which EI is carried out during the day. In the first three columns, the teacher enters the date of instruction, the step number from the teaching plan, and the phase number from the teaching plan. In the remaining columns, the instructor simply enters an "✓" in the box each time they present a natural (N) or supplemental (S) embedded instruction trial to the student during each class, activity, or routine. This information is usually recorded after each trial is presented to the student.

For example, on January 12th, Karen presented the second word set (Step 2) to Jacob and used the "0" second time delay procedure to provide assistance to (Phase I). During the class period, she was able to present a total of six instructional trials, two natural trials, and four supplemental trials.

Figure 5-2

Embedded Instruction Tracking Form

Student: Jacob							Instructor: Karen				
Date/Instructional Condition			Class/Activity/Routine								
Date	Step	Phase	Foods Class								
			N	S	N	S	N	S	N	S	N	S
1/12	2	I	✓✓		✓✓✓							
1/14	2	II	✓		✓✓✓ ✓✓✓							
1/15	2	II	✓✓✓		✓✓✓							
1/16	2	II	✓✓✓		✓✓✓ ✓							
1/17	2	II	✓		✓✓✓ ✓							

To make recording easier, the form can be left at the student's desk and be completed by the instructor during each session. Some instructors have found it helpful to carry a small piece of paper or attach a small paper band to their wrist to record the number of trials provided to the student. Following the session, this information is transferred to the form to allow on-going tracking by the teacher of the number and type of trials provided to the student within and across sessions.

It is typically not necessary to track the number of trials presented to the student each day. Once or twice a week should be sufficient in most cases to ensure that the student is receiving an adequate number of trials. However, the frequency of data collection should be increased if the data suggest that the number of trials presented to the student is declining. The information gathered on the tracking sheet should be reviewed by the teacher at least weekly to ensure that the student is receiving an adequate number of instructional trials to promote efficient learning.

Summary

The quality of EI can be improved by providing the individual who will be carrying out EI by (a) provide training on the implementation of the teaching plan, (b) provide monitoring the instructor's implementation of the teaching plan, and (c) ensure that the instructor provides a sufficient number of learning trials each day. Training should focus on the explicit requirements of successfully implementing the EI teaching plan. The teacher should monitor the instructor's implementation of the plan and the frequency that they present instructional trials regularly. If the instructor deviates from the teaching plan or the instructional trial schedule, he/she should be provided additional training until the frequency of fidelity observations is increased.

Supporting Efficient Student Learning

Once the EI program has been implemented, the teacher may find it necessary to modify or adjust the instructional procedures to ensure that the student continues to learn at the expected rate. Decisions about how to change the instructional procedures should be determined by the patterns in the graphed student performance data. Research has consistently shown that teachers who use data to adjust instructional procedures to meet the student's needs are more effective than those who do not (Haring, Liberty, & White, 1980; Snell & Lloyd, 1991).

Problem Data Patterns

There are four patterns in graphed data that should raise red flags for teachers as they carry out their regular reviews of student performance in EI programs. These are (a) slow improvements in performance, (b) variable performance, (c) flat performance, and (d) decreasing performance. Teachers can use these patterns to help narrow the range of possible explanations for why a student is not making progress as expected in the instructional program (Figure 6-1).

Slow Improvements in Performance

In this pattern, the student's performance is improving at a rate slower than expected. There are many factors that might affect how quickly a student learns a new skill. However, when this problem arises in EI programs, it often means that the instructional task is too difficult for the student. This may occur when the teacher is presenting too many instructional examples at one time or the response that the student is being asked to complete is too hard.

Figure 6-1

Problem Data Patterns in EI Programs

Slow Improvements in Performance

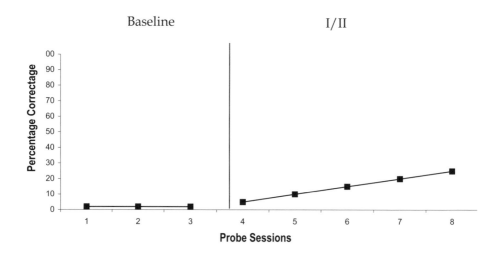

Variable Performance

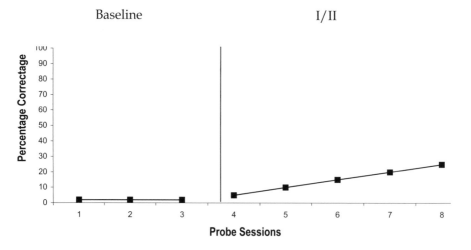

Figure 6-1 continued

Problem Data Patterns in EI Programs

Slow Improvements in Performance

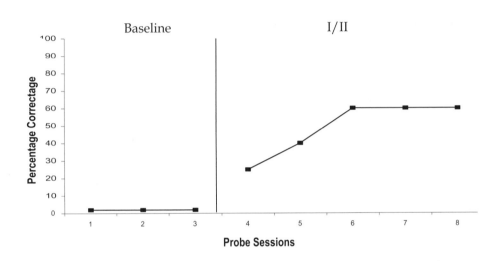

Variable Performance

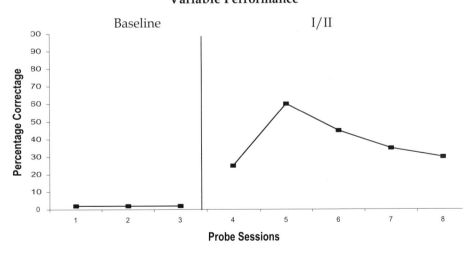

For example, if we saw this pattern with Jacob, it could mean that his teacher had included too many words and symbols in the teaching sets, or that he did not have the necessary discrimination skills to differentiate between the words and symbols. In Lisa's case, this problem could arise because too many symbols had been placed on her communication device, resulting in difficulty discriminating among them. Alternatively, the symbols may not be located in the right position on the device to allow her to successfully depress the button.

Variable Performance Across Probe Sessions

This data pattern can result when the conditions under which the student is learning the new skill are changing from one instructional session to the next while the instructional procedures have not been designed to accommodate this variation. This variation could occur within a class period or across class periods.

For example, Jacob's performance might vary if most of the instructional trials he received were provided during independent seat work times versus during lab activities. His performance might be better during independent seat work activities because there were fewer distractions than during lab activities.

Flat Performance Across Probe Sessions

In this situation, the student's performance initially improves but then stagnates and remains at the same level across multiple probe sessions. There are two likely explanations for this type of pattern. First, the student is making more errors on one or more of the examples included in the teaching plan. The student's overall performance does not improve because he is making mistakes on the same example over and over again. Second, the student may have learned to wait for the teacher's assistance rather than trying to respond independently. For example, if Jacob learned to read "tongs" and "spatula" in the first teaching set, the data would indicate that his performance improved from 0% to 50% correct. If he continued to miss the other two words included in the teaching set, the data pattern would remain flat at 50% across probe sessions. The teacher would see a similar data pattern if Jacob had learned to wait for her assistance on these words rather than trying to read them by himself.

Decreasing Performance Across Probe Sessions

When the student's performance initially improves and then declines after several probe sessions, it often suggests that the student is bored. The instructional procedures will need to be modified to make the instructional task more interesting or more reinforcing for the student to stay engaged in the task. This data pattern can also emerge if the student is not receiving enough instructional trials to maintain performance on the previously learned examples.

Potential Changes in the Instructional Procedures

Modifications or adjustments to the instructional procedures can focus on four key components of the EI program. These include (a) the amount of practice the student is provided, (b) the composition and structure of the teaching set or response, (c) the assistance that the teacher provides to the student, and (d) the strategies used to reinforce the student's unprompted correct responses.

Change the Amount of Practice

There are three possible modifications or adjustments that teachers can make to ensure that students are getting the amount of practice they need to learn the skill. First, the teacher can increase the total number of instructional trials that the student receives during each class period or activity. The teacher may have initially underestimated the number of trials that the student would need to learn a new skill. Second, the teacher may need to focus the majority of instructional trials provided to the student on more difficult examples. As instruction proceeds, it is common to see students learn some of the examples included in the set more quickly than others. When this occurs the teacher might note what kinds of examples the students errs on, and then focus subsequent instructional trials on similar examples.

Finally, the teacher may need to modify the teaching procedures to ensure that the student receives a consistent number of instructional trials each day. A student's learning may be hampered when he receives 10 presentations of the teaching set on Monday, 3 presentations on Tuesday, 1 presentation on Wednesday, and so on.

Change the Teaching Examples or Response

Student performance data may suggest that the teacher should modify the teaching set or alter the specific response that the student is required to make during instructional trials. Experience suggests that there are four possible changes that the teacher might make to improve student learning. First, the teacher may reduce or increase the total number of examples included in the teaching set. Teachers would typically reduce the number of examples included in the teaching set when a student's rate of learning did not match expectations. The objective is to reduce the difficulty of the instructional task for the student and to increase his overall level of success during instructional sessions. Conversely, the teacher may increase the number of examples in the teaching set if it is too easy for the student or if the student is becoming bored with the instructional task. The goal is to make sure that the instructional task stays interesting and challenging to the student.

Second, the teacher might reorganize the teaching sets so that difficult examples are spread out over instructional sessions. For example, if the student is making a large number of errors on three examples included in a teaching set, the teacher might reorganize the set so that the two most difficult examples are taken out of the set, and then reintroduced one at a time as the student's performance improved.

Third, the teacher can change the instructional materials to help the student learn difficult examples. For example, in a foods class the teacher might initially pair the written words or symbols with pictures of the objects. After the student is consistently reading the word or symbol name when presented with the picture, the teacher might delay the presentation of the picture to give the student an opportunity to read the word independently.

Finally, the teacher can simplify or modify the expected response so that it matches the student's ability. This might mean changing the type of response that the student makes during instructional trials. For example, in the foods class a student could point to the object when shown the written word or symbol rather than reading it aloud. The teacher could also develop an alternative response that achieves the same outcome for the student. Thus in the foods class, the teacher could require the student to complete recipes using photographs of the required steps rather than reading a written recipe.

Change Assistance Strategies

Finally, the teacher might alter the response prompting and fading procedures being used to provide assistance to the student. For example, if Jacob consistently made a large number of errors when the teacher moved from the 0-second delay to the 3-second delay, the teacher might shorten the delay interval or change to a progressive time-delay procedure that allows the delay interval to be gradually increased across trials or sessions. Similarly, if the data suggested that Lisa was becoming prompt-dependent in learning to activate her communication device, the teacher might switch to a constant time-delay procedure to reinforce her self-initiated responses.

Change the Reinforcement Strategy

The final component of the teaching plan that often must be adjusted are the reinforcement procedures. These changes can ensure that the student is provided adequate feedback about the unprompted correct responses, thus maintaining student motivation level during instruction. It is common for teachers to change the amount, the frequency, and/or the type of reinforcement provided. In most cases, the teacher will reinforce the student following each unprompted correct response during the initial stages of the instruction. Perhaps the most frequent change is to increase the amount of reinforcement the student receives following a correct response.

Another option is to develop a menu of reinforcers that are available to the student for correct responding during instructional sessions. This change is often needed if the student is losing interest in the instructional task or the particular reinforcer. The teacher might make a variety of activity reinforcers (i.e., listening to a CD, reading a book, feeding the gold fish), any of which available to the student if he is engaged in the instructional task and achieves a certain level of performance during the session.

Troubleshooting Steps

Teachers should use a five-step process to troubleshoot EI programs. These steps are as follows.

1. Assess the consistency of program implementation.
2. Eliminate other contextual explanations for poor student performance.
3. Identify the data pattern.
4. Use the EI troubleshooting matrix to identify a potential hypothesis.
5. Change the teaching plan.

Step 1: Assess the Consistency of Program Implementation

The teacher should assure that the staff is consistently implementing the teaching plan before significant efforts are made to change the procedures. Poor student performance may result when the person carrying out the plan does not consistently present the controlling prompt across instructional trials or sessions. Similarly, the rate of learning may be impacted if different staff members use different procedures to teach the skill to the student.

The way to avoid this problem is for the teacher to regularly observe and provide feedback to staff about their implementation of the EI program (as described earlier). The teacher should ensure that the program is being implemented correctly for at least two consecutive observations before any changes in the teaching plan are considered.

Step 2: Eliminate Other Contextual Explanations

Once the teacher is confident that the teaching plan is being implemented correctly, he/she should make sure that other contextual problems are not negatively impacting the student's performance. For example, the number of instructional trials presented to a student could be affected by changes in the routines or activities of the general education class. Other factors, such as student health problems, can also impact how quickly a student learns a skill. The teacher should eliminate these factors as potential reasons for a student's performance before the EI program is altered.

Step 3: Identify the Data Pattern

Once the teacher is sure that the student's performance is not due to other contextual factors, the teacher should identify whether the student's performance data indicates (a) slow improvements in performance, (b) variable performance, (c) flat performance, or (d) decreasing performance (see Figure 6-1). It is recommended that this decision be based on data from 10 consecutive probe sessions. This amount of data is necessary to establish a clear pattern in the student's performance.

Step 4: Use the Troubleshooting Matrix to Identify a Potential Hypothesis

Once a consistent pattern in the student's performance has been identified, the teacher might consult the EI Troubleshooting Matrix to develop one or more hypotheses about why the student is not making adequate progress (Table 6-1). The matrix provides a general guide for teachers to determine which components of the teaching plan should be changed. The teacher can develop a hypothesis by examining the EI Tracking Sheet and EI Probe Sheet, and observing the student during instruction. An examination of the tracking sheet allows the teacher to assess whether the student is receiving a consistent number of instructional trials each day and whether the amount of practice opportunities needs to be increased.

The teacher should also examine the raw data from the Probe Sheet to identify whether the student is having problems with specific examples included in the teaching plan and, if possible, to identify the type of error(s) that the student is making. If specific error patterns are seen in the raw data, this information can help the teacher identify ways to modify the instructional materials presented to the student or the type of assistance he is provided during instruction.

Finally, the teacher should observe the student's behavior. This will allow the teacher to assess the effectiveness of the assistance and reinforcement strategies for the student.

Once a specific hypothesis for the student's performance has been developed, the teacher should discuss it with the student's general education teacher and with other individuals implementing the EI program to obtain a consensus on (a) what is causing the student's problems and (b) any specific changes that should be made to the teaching plan.

Step 5: Change the Teaching Plan

The teacher should complete a new teaching plan form. The changes should be reviewed with the individual implementing the program, with additional training provided as necessary to ensure that the new procedures are implemented correctly and consistently. Finally, the teacher should note when the changes in teaching plan are put into place on the graph of the student's probe performance.

Summary

No teaching plan is perfect. The teacher should continuously review and adjust the teaching procedures to reflect the student's performance and changes in the general education class. The focus should be on ensuring that the student is making continuous progress in acquiring the skill. This can be accomplished by using student performance data to identify potential problems, developing a hypothesis about why the problem is occurring, and then adjusting one or more components of the teaching plan. As with all aspects of EI, adjustments to the teaching plan should be done collaboratively by the student's IEP team members.

Table 6-1
Troubleshooting Matrix

Data Pattern	Possible Modifications			
	Amount of Practice	Teaching Examples or Response	Assistance Strategies	Reinforcement Strategies
Slow Improvement in Performance *Potential problem: Instructional task is too difficult for the student.*	Increase number of instructional trials.	Reduce the number of examples in the set. Simplify the response or develop an alternative response.	Change the controlling prompt to provide more assistance.	Increase the amount of reinforcement for unprompted responses. Increase the frequency of reinforcement for unprompted responses.
Variable Performance *Potential problem: Instructional procedures are not compatible with all variations in the on-going routines or activities.*	Ensure that a consistent number of trials are presented across sessions.	Change the teaching examples or response to ensure that it is compatible with the ongoing routines and activities.	Change the instructional cues or controlling prompt to ensure that they are compatible with the ongoing routines and activities.	Increase the amount of reinforcement for unprompted responses. Increase the frequency of reinforcement for unprompted responses.

Table 6-1 continued

Data Pattern	Possible Modifications			
	Amount of Practice	Teaching Set or Response	Assistance Strategies	Reinforcement Strategies
Flat Performance *Potential problems: Student is making consistent errors on specific examples.* *Student is becoming dependent on the controlling prompt.*	Provide additional instruction trials on difficult examples.	Reduce the number of difficult examples in the set. Change the instructional materials to highlight the critical features of difficult examples.	Modify the assistance procedure to provide more assistance to the student and reduce error rates. Change the fading procedure to reflect student performance and the skill.	Increase the amount of reinforcement for unprompted responses. Increase the frequency of reinforcement for unprompted responses.
Decreasing Performance *Potential problem: Student is bored because the instructional task is too easy.*	Increase number of instructional trials.	Increase the number of examples included in the teaching set. Increase the difficulty of the examples included in the teaching set.	Change the controlling prompt to provide less assistance.	Develop a menu of reinforcers and vary them across sessions. Increase the amount of reinforcement for unprompted responses. Increase the frequency of reinforcement for unprompted responses.

References

Alwell, M., Hunt, P., Goetz, L., & Sailor, W. (1989). Teaching generalized communication behaviors within interrupted behavior chain contexts. *Journal of the Association for Persons with Severe Handicaps, 14,* 91-100.

Bambara, L. M., & Warren, S. F. (1992). Massed trials revisited: Appropriate applications in functional skill training. In R. A. Gable & S. F. Warren (Eds.), *Strategies for teaching students with mild to severe mental retardation* (pp. 165-190). Baltimore: Paul H. Brookes.

Bambara, L. M., Warren, S. F., & Komisar, S. (1988). The individualized curriculum sequencing model: Effects on skill acquisition and generalization. *Journal of the Association of Persons with Severe Handicaps, 13,* 8-19.

Barbetta, P. M., Heward, W. L., Bradely, D. M., & Miller, A. D. (1994). Effects of immediate and delayed error correction on the acquisition and maintenance of sight words by students with developmental disabilities. *Journal of Applied Behavior Analysis, 27,* 177-178.

Barbetta, P. M., Heron, T. E., & Heward, W. L. (1993). Effects of active student response during error correction on the acquisition, maintenance, and generalization of sight words by students with developmental disabilities. *Journal of Applied Behavior Analysis, 26,* 111-119.

Bates, P., & Renzaglia, A. (1982). Language instruction with a profoundly retarded adolescent: The use of a table game in acquisition of verbal labeling skills. *Education and Training in Mental Retardation, 5,* 13-22.

Batu, S., Ergenekon, Y., Erbas, D., & Akmanoglu, N. (2004). Teaching pedestrian skills to individuals with developmental disabilities. *Journal of Behavioral Education, 13,* 147-164

Brophy, J. E., & Good, T. L. (1986). Teacher behavior and student achievement. In M. C. Wittrock (Ed.), *Handbook of research on teacher* (3rd ed., pp. 328-375). New York: MacMillan.

Carter, E. W., & Kennedy, C. H. (2006). Promoting access to the general curriculum using peer support strategies. *Research and Practice for Persons with Severe Disabilities, 31,* 284-292.

Collins, B. C., Branson, T. A., Hall, M., & Rankin, S. W. (2001). Teaching secondary students with moderate disabilities in an inclusive academic classroom setting. *Journal of Developmental and Physical Disabilities, 13,* 41-59.

Colyer, S. P., & Collins, B. C. (1996). Using natural cures within prompt levels to teach the next dollars strategy to students with disabilities. *The Journal of Special Education, 30,* 305-318.

Cuvo, A. J., Jacobi, L, & Sipko, R. (1981). Teaching laundry skills to mentally retarded students. *Education and Training in Mental Retardation, 16,* 54-64.

Demchak, M. (1990). Response prompt and fading methods: A review. *American Journal on Mental Retardation, 94,* 603-615.

Downing, J. E. (1996). *Including students with severe and multiple disabilities in typical classrooms: Practical strategies for teachers.* Baltimore: Paul H. Brookes.

Doyle, P. M., Wolery, M., Ault, M. J., & Gast, D. L. (1988). System of least prompts: A literature review of procedural parameters. *The Journal of the Association for Persons with Severe Handicaps, 13,* 28-40.

Duker, P. C., & Morsink. H. (1984). Acquisition and cross-setting generalization of manual signs with severely retarded individuals. *Journal of Applied Behavior Analysis, 17,* 93-103.

Dunlap, L. K., & Dunlap, G. (1987). Using task variation to motivate handicapped students. *TEACHING Exceptional Children, 19,* 16-19.

Etzel, B. C., & LeBlanc, J. M. (1979). The simplest treatment alternative: The law of parsimony applied to choosing appropriate instructional control and errorless-learning procedures for the difficult-to-teach child. *Journal of Autism and Developmental Disorders, 9,* 361-382.

Fantuzzo, J., & Atkins, M. (1992). Applied behavior analysis for educators: Teacher centered and classroom based. *Journal of Applied Behavior Analysis, 25,* 37-42.

Farlow, L. J., & Snell, M. E. (1994). *Making the most of student performance data.* Washington, DC: American Association on Mental Retardation.

Ford, A., Schnorr, R., Meyer, L., Davern, L., Black, J., & Dempsey, P. (1989). *The Syracuse Community-Referenced Curriculum Guide.* Baltimore: Paul H. Brookes.

Gee, K., Graham, N., Goetz, L., Oshima, G., & Yoshioka, K. (1991). Teaching students to request the continuation of a routine activities by using time delay and decreasing physical assistance in the context of chain interruption. *Journal of the Association for Persons with Severe Handicaps, 16,* 154-167.

Giangreco, M. F., Dennis, R., Cloninger, C. J., Edelman, S., & Schattman, R. (1993). "I've counted Jon": Transformational experiences of teachers educating students with disabilities. *Exceptional Children, 59,* 359-372.

Giangreco, M. F., Edelman, S., & Broer, S. M. (2001). Respect, appreciation, and acknowledgement of paraprofessionals who support students with disabilities. *Exceptional Children, 67,* 485-498.

Giangreco, M. F., & Putnam, J. (1991). Supporting the education of students with severe disabilities in regular education environments. In L. H. Meyer, C. A. Peck, & L. Brown (Eds)., *Critical issues in the lives of people with severe disabilities* (pp. 245-270). Baltimore: Paul H. Brookes.

Goetz, L., Gee, K., & Sailor, W. (1985). Using a behavior chain interruption strategy to teach communication skills to students with severe disabilities. *Journal of the Association for Persons with Severe Handicaps 10,* 21-30.

Greenwood, C. R., Delquadri, J., & Hall, R. V. (1984). Opportunity to respond and student academic performance. In W. L. Heward, T. E. Heron, J. Trapp-Porter, & D. S. Hill (Eds.), *Focus on behavior analysis in education* (pp. 58-88). Columbus, OH: Charles E. Merrill.

Guess, D., & Helmstetter, E. (1986). Skill cluster instruction and the individualized curriculum sequencing model. In R. H. Horner, L. H. Meyer, & H. D. Bud Fredericks (Eds.), *Education of learners with severe handicaps: Exemplary service strategies* (pp. 221-250). Baltimore: Paul H. Brookes.

Hall, L. J., McClannahan, L. E., & Krantz, P. J. (1995). Promoting independence in integrated classrooms by teaching aides to use activity schedules and decreased prompts. *Education and Training in Mental Retardation and Developmental Disabilities, 30,* 208-217.

Halle, J. W., Baer, D. W., & Spradlin, J. E. (1981). Teachers' generalized use of delay as a stimulus control procedure to increase language use in handicapped children. *Journal of Applied Behavior Analysis, 14,* 389-409.

Halle, J. W., Marshall, A., & Spradlin, J. E. (1979). Time delay: A technique to increase language and facilitate generalization in retarded children. *Journal of Applied Behavior Analysis, 12,* 431-439.

Halvorsen, A. T., & Sailor, W. (1990). Integration of students with severe and profound disabilities. In R. Gaylord-Ross (Ed.), *Issues and Research in Special Education* (pp. 110-172). New York: Teachers College Press.

Haring , N., Liberty, K., & White, O. R. (1980). Rules for data-based strategy decisions in instructional programs: Current research and implications. In W. Sailor, B. Wilcox, & L. Brown (Eds.), *Methods of instruction for severely handicapped learners* (pp. 159-162). Baltimore: Paul H. Brookes.

Harrower, J. (1999). Educational inclusion of children with severe disabilities. *Journal of Positive Behavioral Interventions, 1,* 215-230.

Hart, B., & Risley, T. (1968). Establish use of descriptive adjectives in the spontaneous speech of disadvantaged preschool children. *Journal of Applied Behavior Analysis, 1,* 109-120.

Hart, B, & Risley, T. (1974). Using preschool materials to modify the language of disadvantaged children. *Journal of Applied Behavior Analysis, 7,* 243-256.

Hart, B. & Risley, T. (1975). Incidental teaching of language in the preschool. *Journal of Applied Behavior Analysis, 8,* 411-420.

Hepting, N. H., & Goldstein, H. (1996). What's natural about naturalistic language instruction? *Journal of Early Intervention, 20,* 250-265.

Horner, R. H., McDonnell, J. J., & Bellamy, G. T. (1986). Teaching generalized skills: General case instruction in simulation and community settings. In R. H. Horner, L. H. Meyer & H. D. Fredericks (Eds.), *Education of learners with severe handicaps: Exemplary service strategies* (pp. 289-214). Baltimore: Paul H. Brookes.

Hunt, P., Doering, K., Hirose-Hatae, A., Maier, J., & Goetz, L. (2001). Across-person collaboration to support students with and without disabilities in a general education classroom. *Journal of the Association for Persons with Severe Handicaps, 26,* 240-256.

Hunt, P., & Goetz, L. (1997). Research on inclusive educational programs, practices, and outcomes for students with severe disabilities. *The Journal of Special Education, 31,* 3-29.

Hunt, P., Goetz, L, Alwell, M., & Sailor, W. (1986). Using an interrupted behavior chain strategy to teach generalized communication responses. *Journal of the Association for Persons with Severe Handicaps, 11,* 196-204.

Hunt, P., & McDonnell, J. (2007). Inclusive education. In S. L. Odom, R. H. Horner, M. Snell & J. Blacher (Eds.), *Handbook on Developmental Disabilities* (pp. 269-291). New York: Guilford Press.

Hunt, P., Soto, G., Maier, J., & Doering, K. (2003). Collaborative teaming to support students at risk and students with severe disabilities in general education classrooms. *Exceptional Children, 69,* 315-332.

Jameson, M., & McDonnell, J. (2007). *Embedded constant time delay instruction by peers without disabilities in general education classrooms.* Salt Lake City, UT: Department of Special Education, University of Utah.

Jameson, J. M., McDonnell, J., Johnson, J. W., Riesen, T., & Polychronis, S. (2007). A comparison of one-to-one embedded instruction in the general education classroom and one-to-one massed practice instruction the special education classroom. *Education and Treatment of Children, 30,* 23-44.

Janey, R., & Snell, M. E. (2000). *Modifying schoolwork.* Baltimore: Paul H. Brookes.

Johnson, J. W., & McDonnell, J. (2004). An exploratory study of the implementation of embedded instruction by general educators with students with developmental disabilities. *Education and Treatment of Children, 27,* 46-63.

Johnson, J. W., McDonnell, J., & Holzwarth, V. (2007). *The effects of embedded instruction on students with developmental disabilities in general education Classes: A comparison of constant time-delay and the system of least prompts.* DeKalb, IL: Northern Illinois University.

Johnson, J. W., McDonnell, J., Holzwarth, V., & Berry, R. (2007). *Using embedded instruction to teach students with developmental disabilities in general education classes: a comparison of simultaneous prompting and the system of most prompts.* Dekalb, IL: Northern Illinois University.

Johnson, J. W., McDonnell, J., Holzwarth, V., & Hunter, K. (2004). The efficacy of embedded instruction for students with developmental disabilities enrolled in general education classes. *Journal of Positive Behavioral Interventions, 6,* 214-227.

Jones, G. Y., & Collins, B. C. (1997). Teaching microwave skills to adults with disabilities: Acquisition of nutrition and safety facts presented as nontargeted information. *Journal of Developmental and Physical Disabilities, 9,* 59-78.

Kaiser, A., Hendrickson, J., & Alpert, C. (1991). Milieu language teaching: A second look. In R. Gable (Ed.), *Advances in mental retardation and developmental disabilities* (Vol. 4, pp. 63-92). London: Jessica Kingsley.

Kayser, J. E., Billingsley, F. F., & Neel, R. S. (1986). A comparison of in-context and traditional instructional approaches: Total task, single trial verses backward chaining, multiple trials. *The Journal of The Association for Persons with Severe Handicaps, 11*, 39-38.

King, D., & Mace. F. C. (1990). Acquisition and maintenance of exercise skills under normalized conditions by adults with moderate and severe mental retardation. *Mental Retardation, 28*, 311-318.

Koegel, R. L., O'Dell, M. C., & Koegel, L. K. (1987). A natural language paradigm for nonverbal autistic children, *Journal of Autism and Developmental Disorders, 17*, 187-200.

Losardo, A., & Bricker, D. (1994). Activity-based intervention and direct instruction: A comparison study. *American Journal on Mental Retardation, 98*, 774-765.

Macey, N. G., & Wheeler, J. J. (2000). Acquisition and generalization of activity schedules and the effects on task engagement in a young child with autism in an inclusive preschool classroom. *Education and Training in Mental Retardation and Developmental Disabilities, 35*, 326-335.

McBride, B. J., & Schwartz, I. S. (2003). Effects of teaching early interventionists to use discrete trials during ongoing classroom activities. *Topics in Early Childhood Special Education, 23*, 5-17.

McDonnell, J. (1998). Instruction for students with severe disabilities in general education settings. *Education and Training in Mental Retardation and Developmental Disabilities, 33*, 199-215.

McDonnell, J., Johnson, J. W., Polychronis, S., & Riesen, T. (2002). The effects of embedded instruction on students with moderate disabilities enrolled in general education classes. *Education and Training in Mental Retardation and Developmental Disabilities, 37*, 363-377.

McDonnell, J., Johnson, J. W., Polychronis, S., Riesen, T., Jameson, J. M., & Kercher, K. (2006). A comparison of one-to-one embedded instruction in general education classes with small group instruction in special education classes. *Education and Training in Developmental Disabilities, 41*, 125-138.

Morse, T. E., & Schuster, J. W. (2004). Simultaneous prompting: A review of the literature. *Education and Training in Developmental Disabilities, 39*, 153-168.

Mulligan, M., Lacy, L., & Guess, D. (1982). Effects of massed, distributed and spaced trail training on severely handicapped students' performance. *Journal of the Association for the Severely Handicapped, 7*, 48-61.

Pierce, K., & Schreibman, L. S. (1995). Increasing complex social behavior in children with autism: Effects of peer-implemented pivotal response training. *Journal of Applied Behavior Analysis, 28*, 285-295.

References

Pierce, K., & Schreibman, L. (1997). Multiple peer use of pivotal response training to increase social behaviors of classmates with autism: Results from trained and untrained peers. *Journal of Applied Behavior Analysis, 30,* 157-160.

Polychronis, S. C., McDonnell, J., Johnson, J. W., Riesen, T., & Jameson, M. (2004). A comparison of two trial distribution schedules in embedded instruction. *Focus on Autism and Other Developmental Disabilities, 19,* 140-151.

Reynolds, A. J. (1991). Early schooling of children at risk. *American Educational Research Journal, 28,* 392-442.

Riesen, T., McDonnell, J., Johnson, J. W., Polychronis, S., & Jameson, M. (2003). A comparison of time delay and simultaneous prompting within embedded instruction in general education classes with students with moderate to severe disabilities. *Journal of Behavioral Education, 12,* 241-260.

Rosenshine, B., & Berliner, D. (1978). Academic engage time. *British Journal of Teacher Education, 4,* 3-16.

Rosenshine, B., & Stevens, R. (1986). Teaching functions. In M. C. Wittrock (Ed.), *Handbook on research on teaching* (3rd ed., pp. 376-391). New York: Macmillian.

Rosenthal-Malek, A., & Bloom, A. (1998). Beyond acquisition: Teaching generalization for students with developmental disabilities. In A. Hilton & R. Ringlaben (Eds.), *Best and promising practices in developmental disabilities* (pp. 139-155). Austin, TX: Pro-Ed.

Rule, S., Losardo, A., Dinnebeil, L., Kaiser, A., & Rowland, C. (1998). Translating research on naturalistic instruction into practice. *Journal of Early Intervention, 21,* 283-293.

Ryndak, D. L., & Alper, S. (2003). *Curriculum and instruction for students with significant disabilities in inclusive settings.* Upper Saddle River, NJ: Allyn & Bacon.

Salisbury, C. L., Evans, I. M., & Palombaro, M. M. (1997). Collaborative problem-solving to promote the inclusion of young children with significant disabilities in primary grades. *Exceptional Children, 63,* 195-209.

Schepis, M. M., Reid, D. H., Ownbey, J., & Parsons, M. B. (2001). Training support staff to embed teaching within natural routines of young children with disabilities in an inclusive preschool. *Journal of Applied Behavior Analysis, 34,* 313-327.

Schuster, J. W., Hemmeter, M. L., & Ault, M. J. (2001). Instruction of students with moderate and severe disabilities in elementary classrooms. *Early Childhood Research Quarterly, 16,* 329-341.

Schuster, J. W., Morse, T. E., Ault, M. J., Doyle, P. M., Crawford, M. R., & Wolery, M. (1998). Constant time delay with chained tasks: A review of the literature. *Education and Treatment of Children, 21,* 74-106.

Schwartz, I. S., Anderson, S. R., & Halle, J. W. (1989). Training teachers to use naturalistic time delay: Effects on teacher behavior and on the language use of students. *The Journal of the Association for Persons with Severe Handicaps, 14*, 48-57.

Smith, R. L., Collins, B. C., Schuster, J. W., & Kleinert, H. (1999). Teaching table cleaning skills to secondary students with moderate/severe disabilities: Facilitating observation learning during instruction downtime. *Education and Training in Mental Retardation and Developmental Disabilities, 34*, 342-252.

Snell, M. E. (2007). Effective instructional practices. *TASH Connections, 33 (3/4)*, 8-12.

Snell, M. E., & Brown, F. (2000). *Instruction of students with severe disabilities* (5th ed.). Upper Saddle River, NJ: Merrill.

Snell, M. E., & Lloyd, B. H. (1991). A study of the effects of trend, variability, frequency, and form of data on teachers' judgments about progress and their decisions about program change. *Research in Developmental Disabilities, 12*, 41-62.

Test, D. W., Grossi, T., & Keul, P. (1988). A functional analysis of the acquisition and maintenance of janitorial skills in a competitive work setting. *The Journal of the Association for Persons with Severe Handicaps, 13*, 1-7.

U. S. Department of Education. (2002). *Twenty-fourth annual Report to Congress on the implementation of the Individuals With Disabilities Education Act*. Washington, DC: Author.

VanDerHeyden, A. M., Snyder, P., Smith, A., Sevin, B., & Longwell, J. (2005). Effects of complete learning trails on child engagement. *Topics in Early Childhood Special Education, 25*, 81-94.

Villa, R. A., & Thousand, J. S. (2000). Collaborative teaming: A powerful tool in school restructuring. In R. A. Villa & J. S. Thousand (Eds.), *Restructuring for caring and effective education: Piecing the puzzle together* (2nd ed., pp. 254-291). Baltimore: Paul H. Brookes.

Warren, S., McQuarter, R., & Rogers-Warren, A. (1984). The effects of mands and models on the speech of unresponsive socially isolated children. *Journal of Speech and Hearing, 49*, 43-52.

Werts, M. G., Wolery, M., Holcombe, A., Vassilaros, M. A., & Billings, S. S. (1992). Efficacy of transition-based teaching with instructive feedback. *Education and Treatment of Children, 15*, 320-334.

Westling, D. L., & Fox, L. (2004). *Teaching students with severe disabilities* (3rd ed). Upper Saddle River, NJ: Merrill.

Wilcox, B., & Bellamy, G. T. (1987). *A comprehensive guide to the activities catalog: An alternative curriculum for youth and adults with severe disabilities.* Baltimore: Paul H. Brookes.

Winterling, V., Dunlap, G., O'Neill, R. E. (1987). The influence of task variation on the aberrant behaviors of autistic children. *Education and Treatment of Children, 10*, 105-119.

Wolery, M., Anthony, L., Caldwell, N. K., Snyder, E. D., & Morgante, J. D. (2002). Embedding and distributing constant time delay in circle time and transitions. *Topics in Early Childhood Special Education, 22,* 14-25.

Wolery, M., Anthony, L., Snyder, E. D., Werts, M., & Katzenmeyer, J. (1997). Training elementary teachers to embed instruction during classroom activities. *Education and Treatment of Children,* 20(1), 40-58.

Wolery, M., Ault, M. J., & Doyle, P. M. (1992). *Teaching students with moderate to severe disabilities: Use of response prompting strategies.* New York: Longman.

Wolery, M., Bailey, D. B., & Sugai, G. M. (1988). *Effective teaching: Principles and procedures of applied behavior analysis with exceptional students.* Upper River, NJ: Allyn and Bacon.

York-Barr, J., Schultz, T., Doyle, M. B., Kronberg, R., & Crossett, S. (1996). Inclusive schooling in St. Cloud. *Remedial and Special Education, 17,* 92-105.

APPENDIX A
Blank Forms

Baseline Probe Form

Student: **Teacher:**

Instructional Cue:

Example	+/0	Prompt	+/0	Prompt	+/0	Prompt

Trial Distribution Planning Form

		Class/Activity/ Routine					Total Opportunities
Student:				**Teacher:**			
Potential Teaching Opportunities							
Natural Instructional Trials							
Supplemental Instructional Trials	Activity Transitions (Opening to lecture; lecture to individual or group activities; going to Lab)						
	Natural Breaks in Activities (Lab)						
	Management Tasks (Roll; distribution of graded assignments)						
	Independent Work						
Potential Opportunities							

Embedded Instruction TeachingForm

Student:
Instructional Objective:

Natural Instruction Opportunities	Supplemental Instruction Opportunities

Presentation Sequence:

Assistance Strategy:

Reinforcement Procedures:

Error Correction Procedures:

Illustrative Probe Form

Student:									Teacher:		
Example/Item	Date										
Percentage Correct											

Notes. V = Verbal; M = Model; G = Gesture/Point; P = Prime; F = Full Physical.

Illustrative Program Monitoring Form

Student:		EI Program Step:		
Instructor:		**Date:**		

Trial Program Step					
Percentage Correct (Total Correct Steps/ Total Steps x 100)					

Embedded Instruction Tracking Form

Student:			Instructor:									
Date/Instructional Condition			Class/Activity/Routine									
Date	Step	Phase	N	S	N	S	N	S	N	S	N	S

APPENDIX B
Training Manual

Peer Tutor Training Manual

I want to teach you how to **Embed** instruction into the ongoing activities and routines of your general education class using a **Constant Time Delay Procedure**. Before we get started, lets look at two of the terms used here and talk about them for a second.

Embed. To embed instruction simply means that we will teach, through one-to-one teaching, ceramics terms to Ella in her Arts and Crafts class. In order to do this we want to be sure that we don't interrupt the usual activities in the class to complete Ella's teaching. The way we will avoid this is by **embedding** the teaching into times when both you and Ella do not have any demands from the teacher. For example, if the teacher is calling roll or taking time to hand back assignments that were graded, that might be a good time to do a couple of teaching trials. It would not be appropriate for you to teach Ella while the teacher was giving a lecture or demonstrating something to the class! Let's take some time to identify some good time for instruction:

Yes	No	Transitions (Moving from one activity to another)
Yes	No	Parallel instruction
Yes	No	Teacher Lecture Time
Yes	No	Testing/Assessment time
Yes	No	Free time
Yes	No	Independent Activity
Yes	No	Other?_____

It will be up to you to decide when you will provide instruction during the class. It is very important, however, that in each class when you are teaching, you provide at least **three trials** for each of the items that Ella will be learning.

Constant time delay (CTD). Constant time delay is an instructional procedure that is both natural and intuitive. You used some of the steps already when you taught Ella before this training! It is easy to use! It is designed to ensure that students with disabilities get the immediate feedback on the skills they are learning in a systematic and controlled way. It also ensures that they make very few errors while they are learning the material. The basic process is to:

1) Select on opportunity to teach (remember…three times per item in each class).
2) Get the student's attention.
3) Present the item to be learned (flashcard).
4) Give teaching request.

---

5) Provide time for a response.
6) Provide feedback.
7) Provide praise/correction.
8) Record data.

There are two types of delay we need to go through. The first is the 0-second time delay. The second is a 3-second time delay. Let's look at both.

Let's look at an example of 0-second time delay.

Select on opportunity to teach (remember…at least three times per item in each class).	Remember … choose times that do not cause disruption or distraction during your class.
Get the student's attention.	"Ella, look at the card."
Present the item to be learned (flashcard).	Show Ella the flashcard.
Give teaching request.	"Ella, _____means _____?"
Provide time for a response.	In this case we don't provide any time. We provide the answer immediately. This makes sure that Ella does not make any errors yet (0 second time delay).
Provide feedback.	Ella, _____means _____. Example: Ella, wedging means to mix clay. You tell her the correct answer and make her repeat it back to you exactly.
Provide praise/correction.	If Ella repeated correctly, you would say, "Good job, Ella. That is right." If Ella did not repeat what you had said then you'd say "No. Ella , _____ means _____."
Record the data.	Mark on a data collection sheet if she repeated correctly (+) or not (-).

Let's look at an example of 3-second time delay.

Select on opportunity to teach (remember…at least three times per item in each class).	Remember…choose times that do not cause disruption or distraction during your class.
Get the student's attention.	"Ella, look at the card."
Present the item to be learned (flashcard).	Show Ella the flashcard.
Give teaching request.	"Ella, _____ means _____ ?"
Provide time for a response.	In this case you provide 3 seconds. This gives Ella time to respond.
Provide praise/correction.	If Ella answered correctly, you would say, "Good job, Ella. That is right." If Ella did not answer correctly then you'd say No. Ella , _____ means _____."
Record the data.	Mark on a data collection sheet if she answered correctly or not (before correction).

Let's practice a few times. I will play Ella and you provide me with instruction.